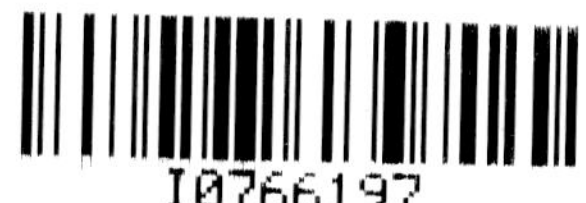

Edited by Sabrine Micha Na
Layout by Vagner Lopes
Photographs by Salenta

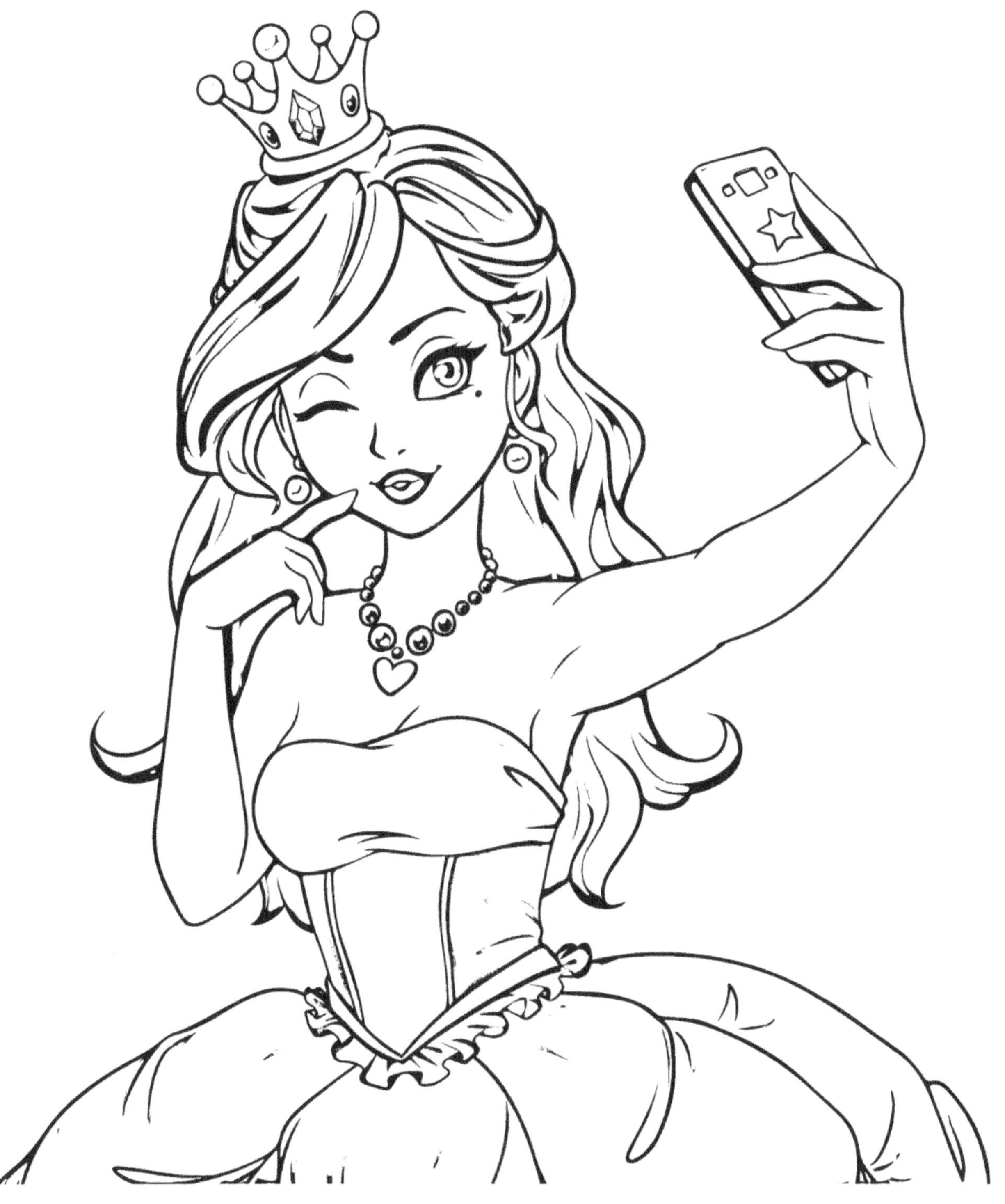

This book belongs to :

....

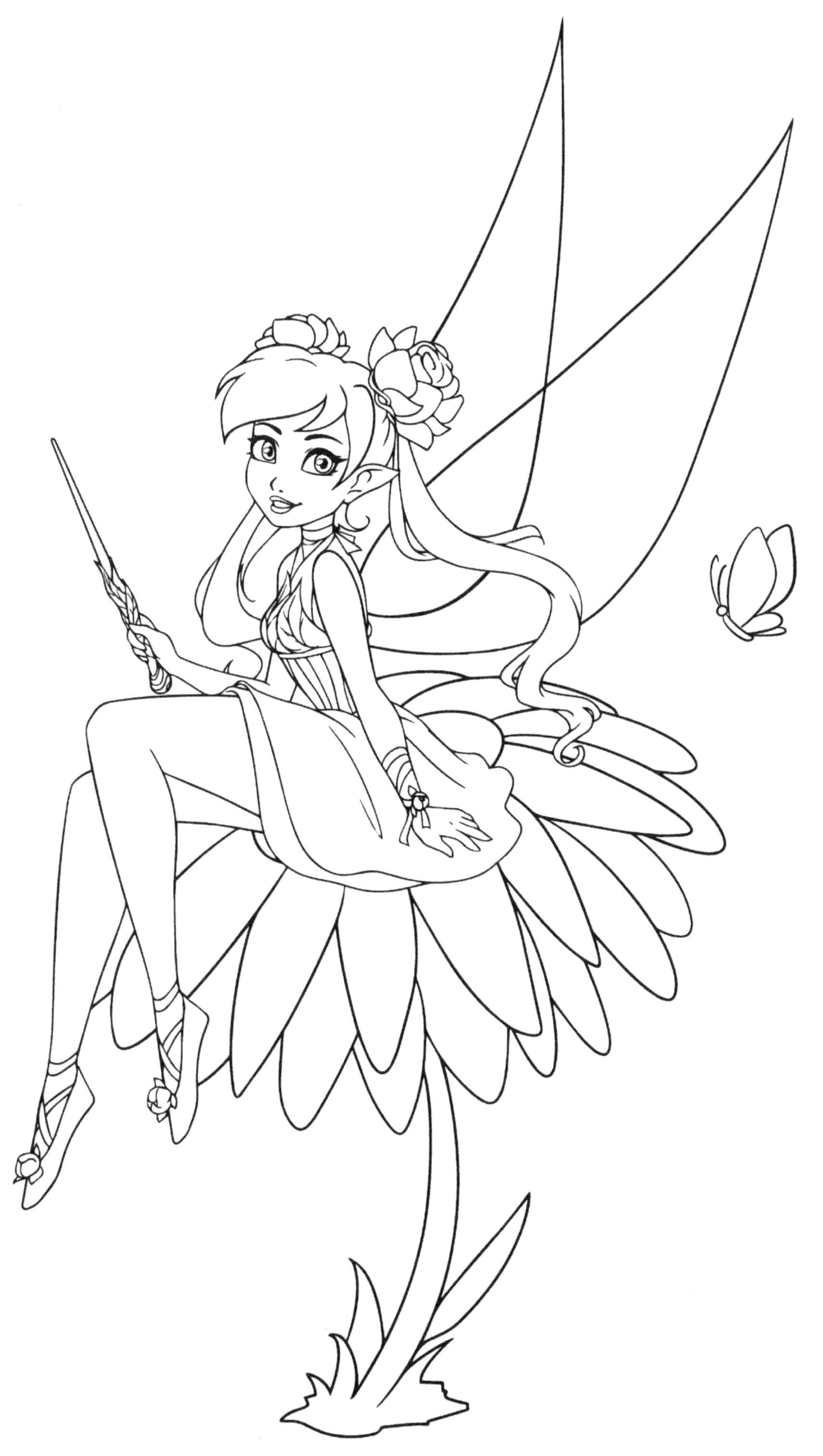

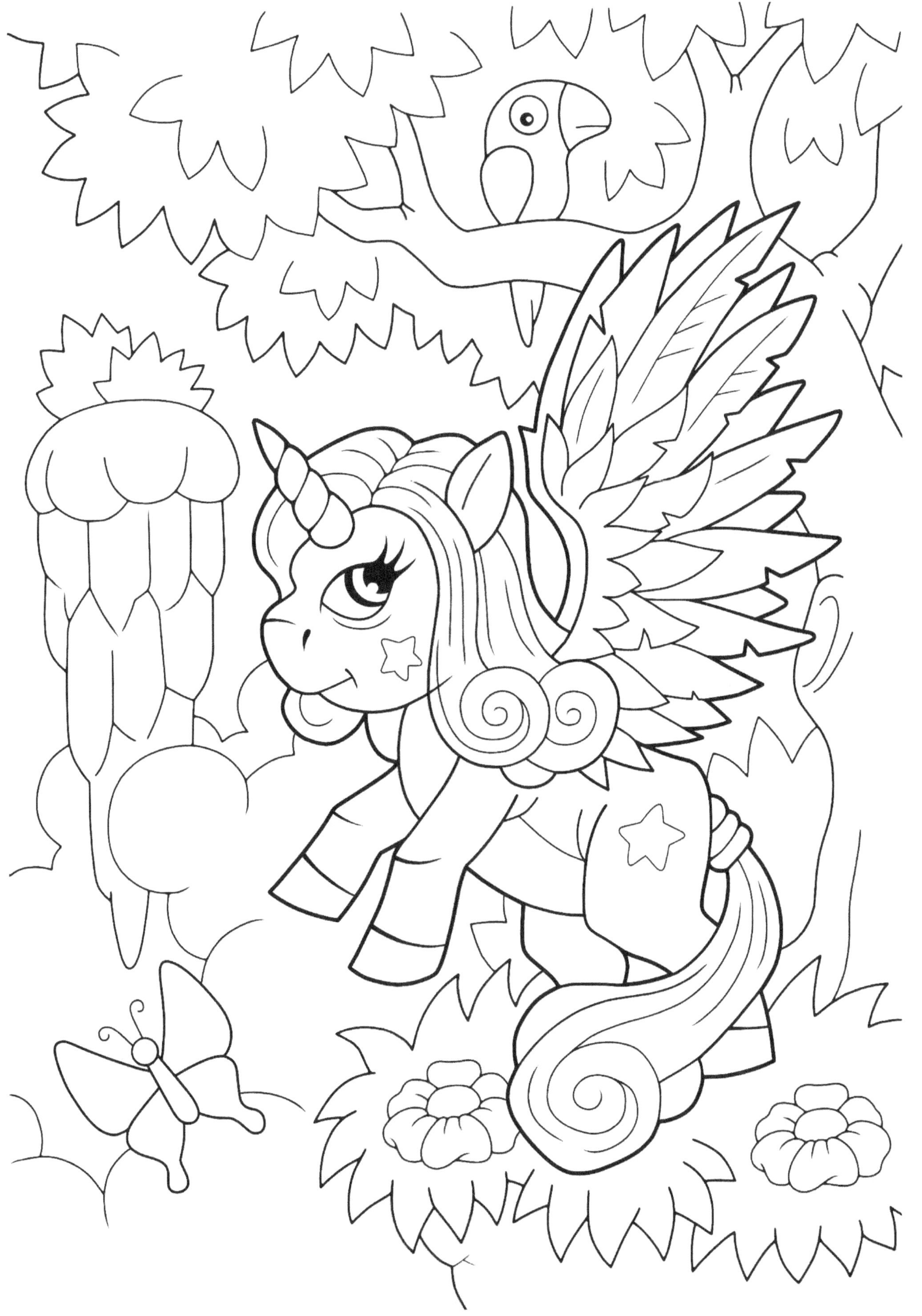

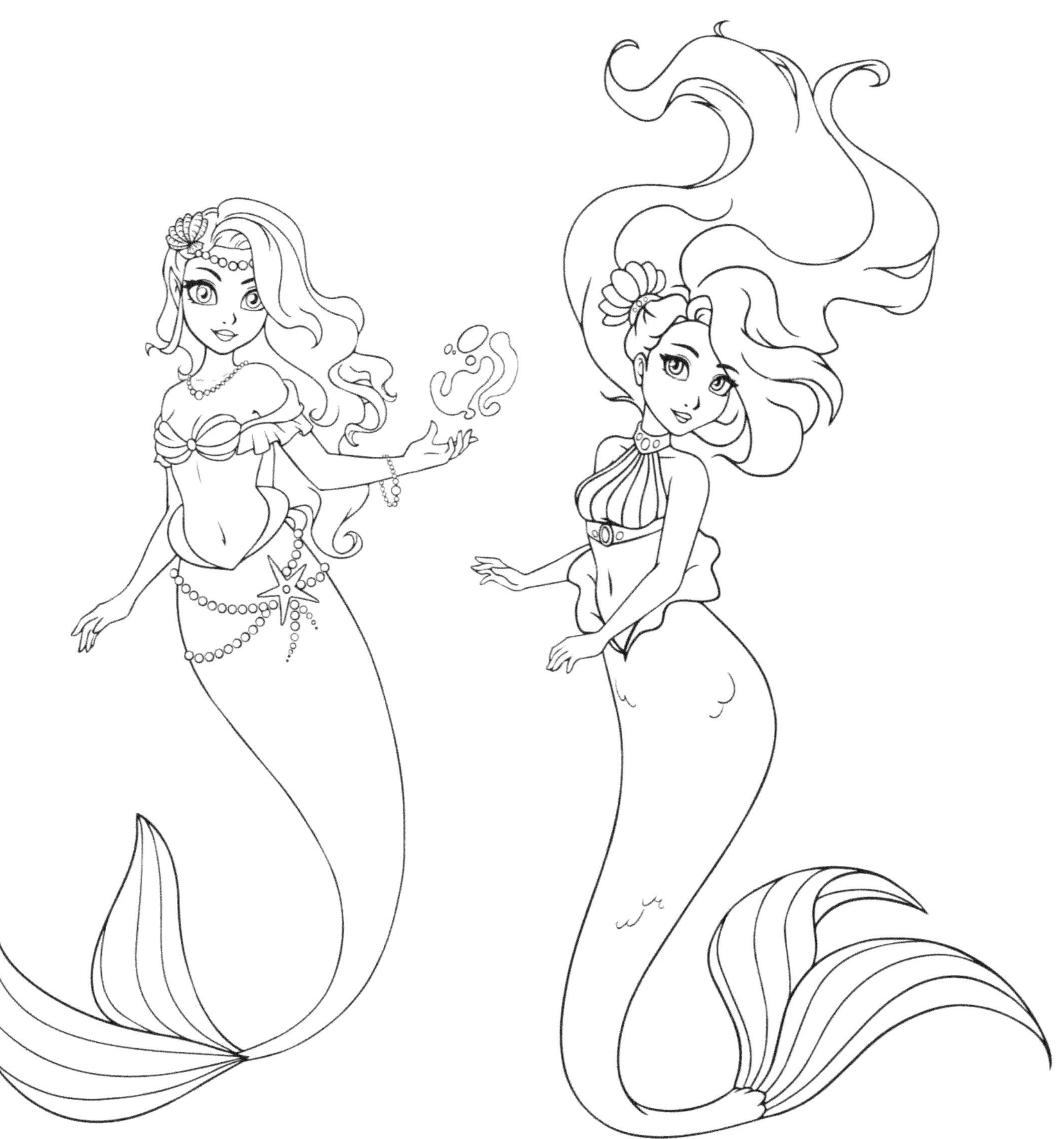

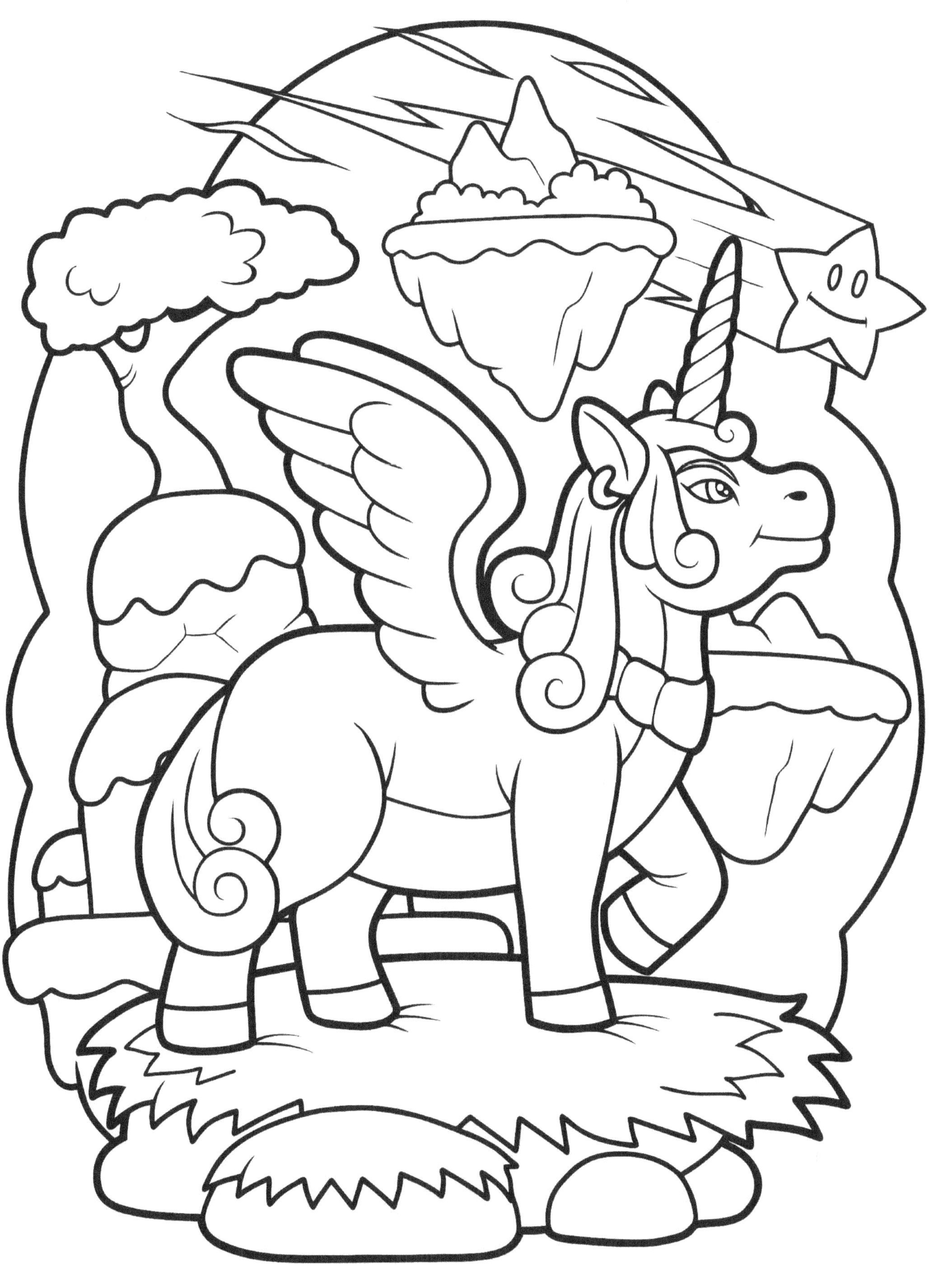

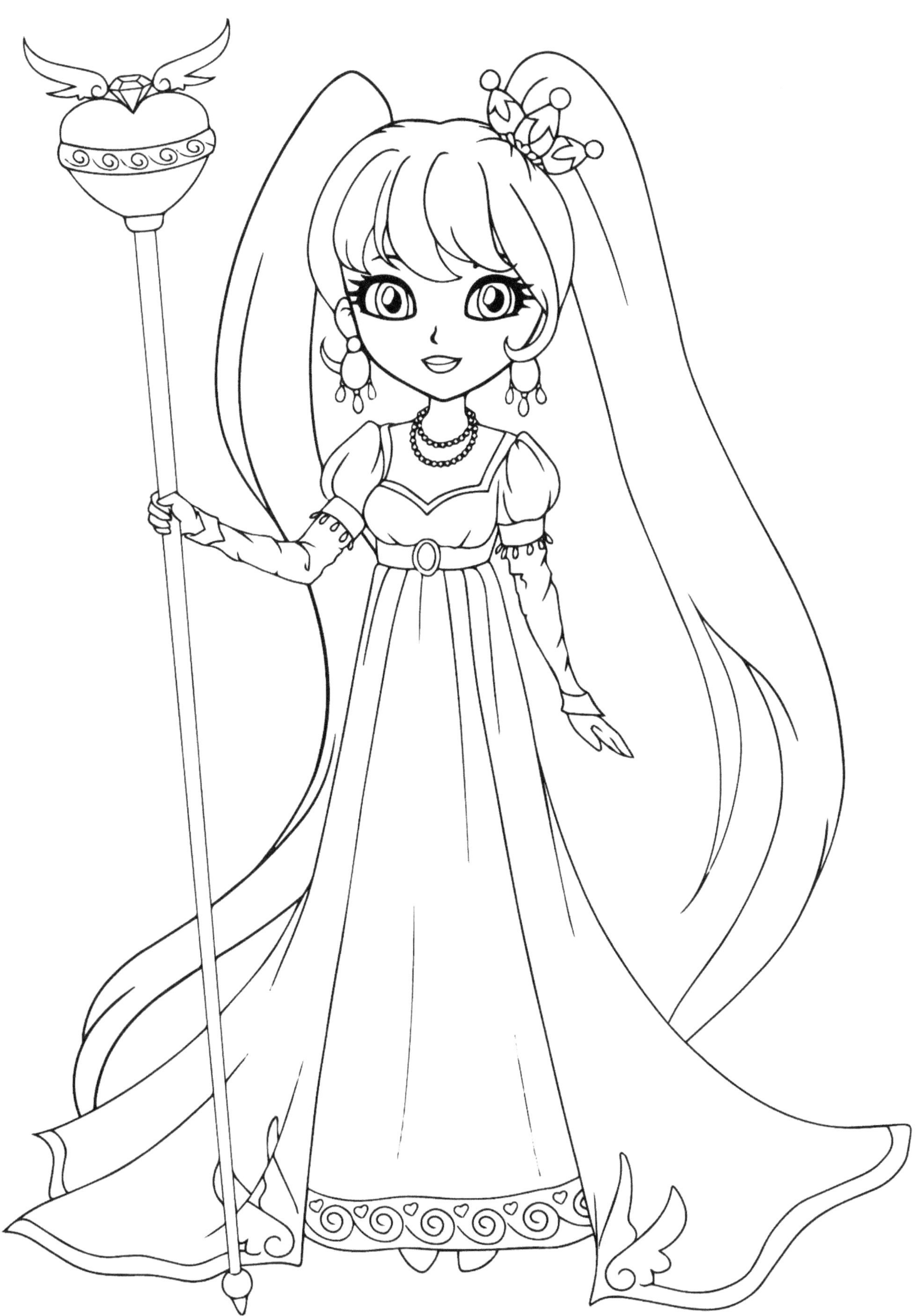

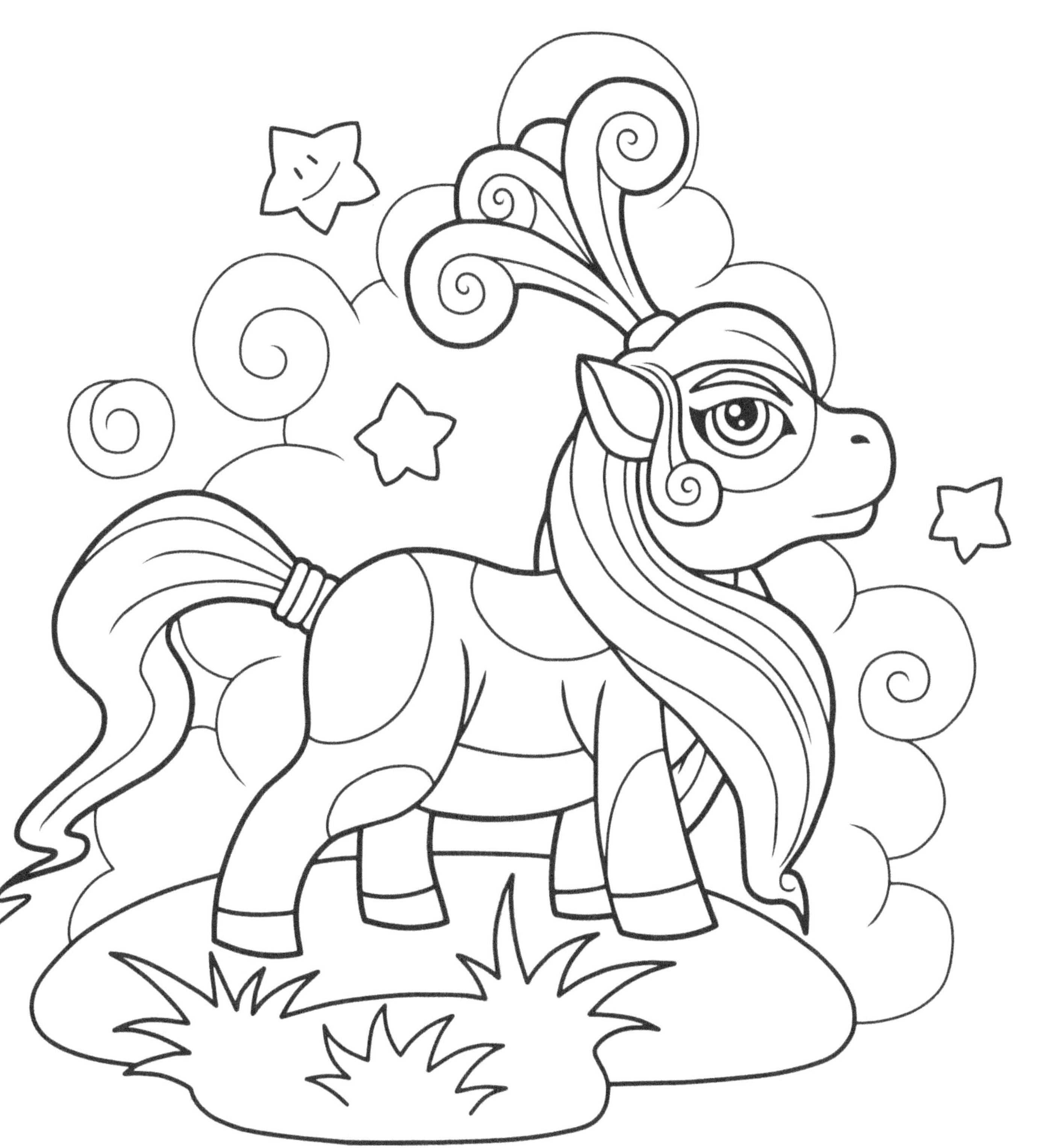

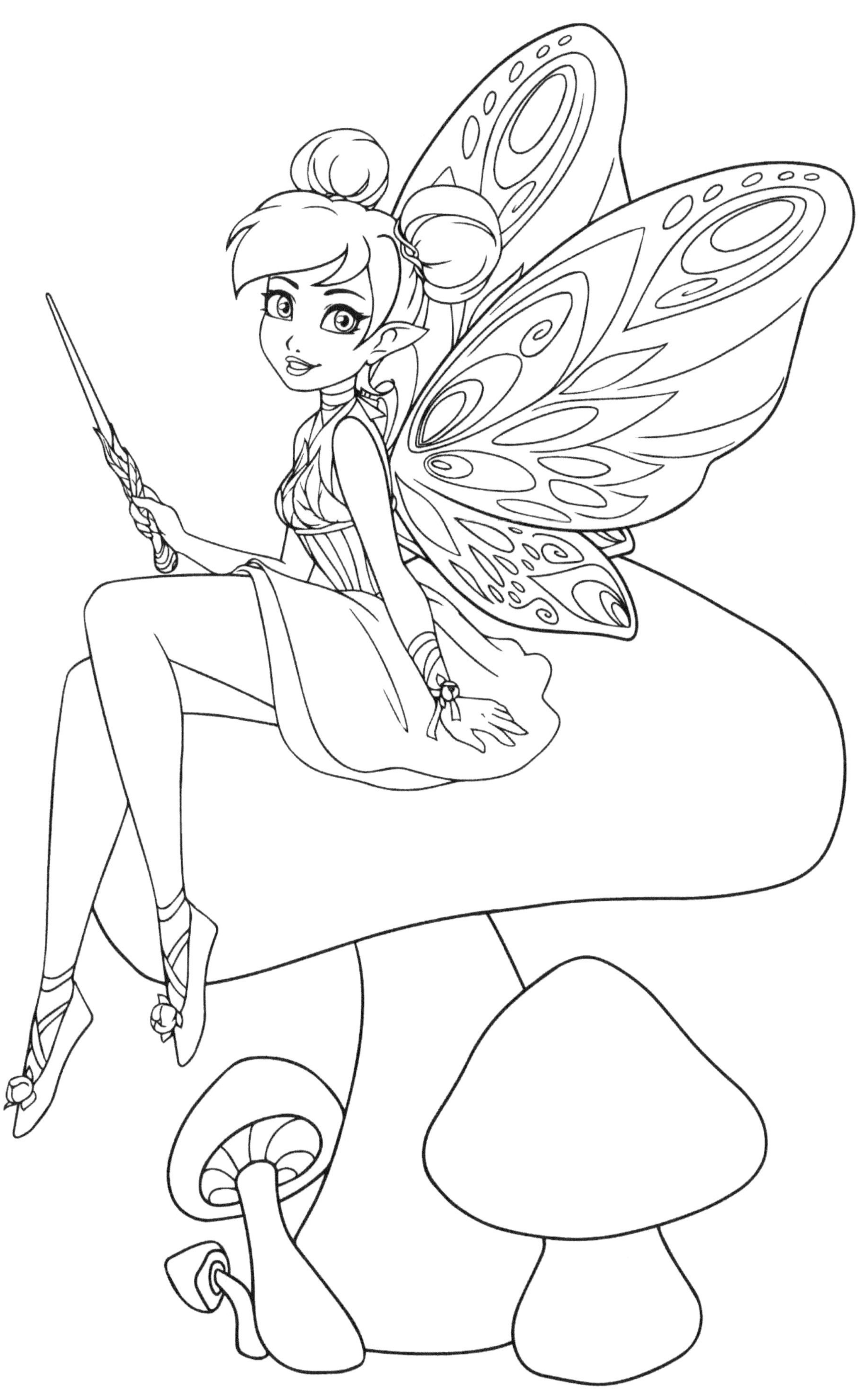

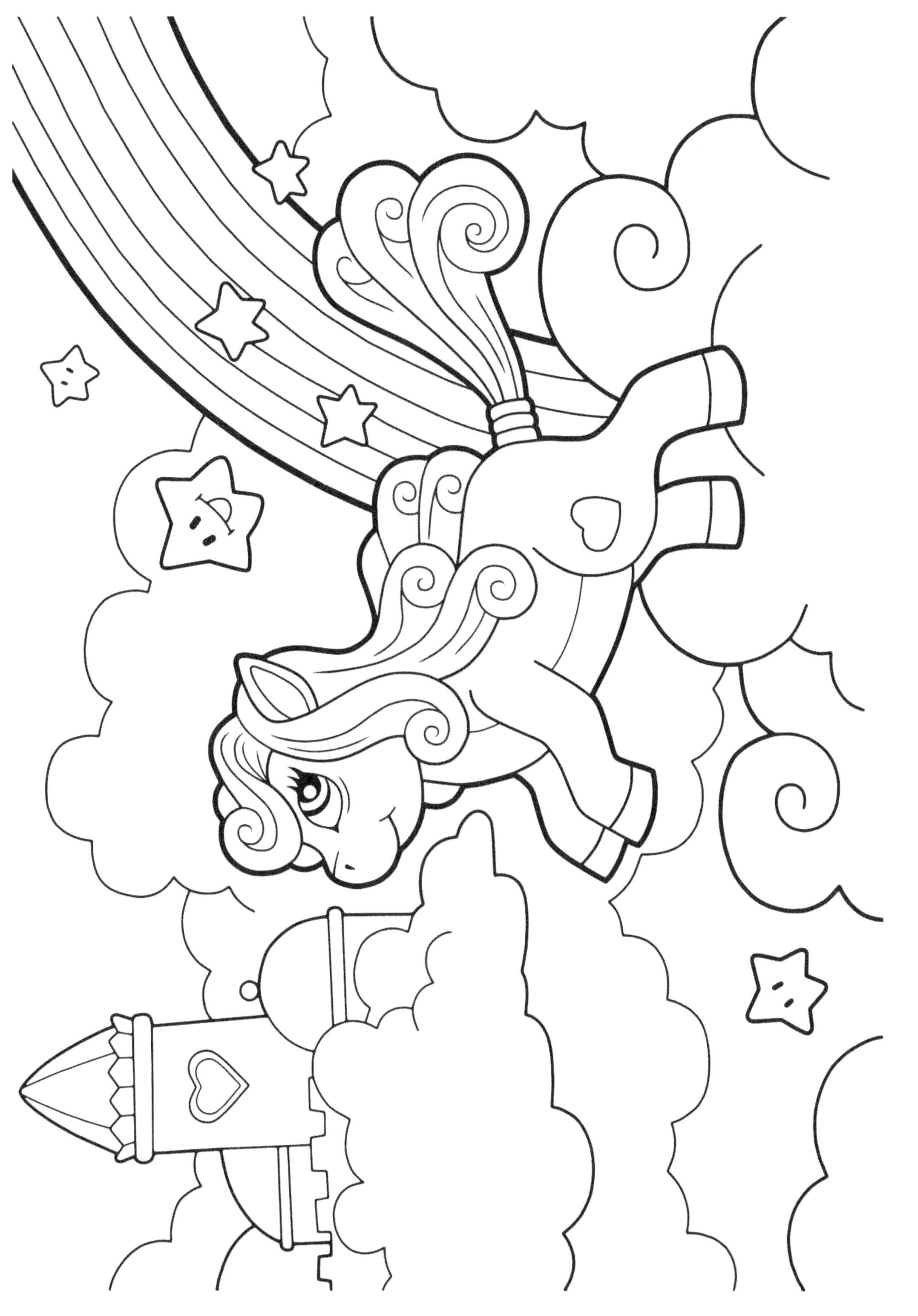

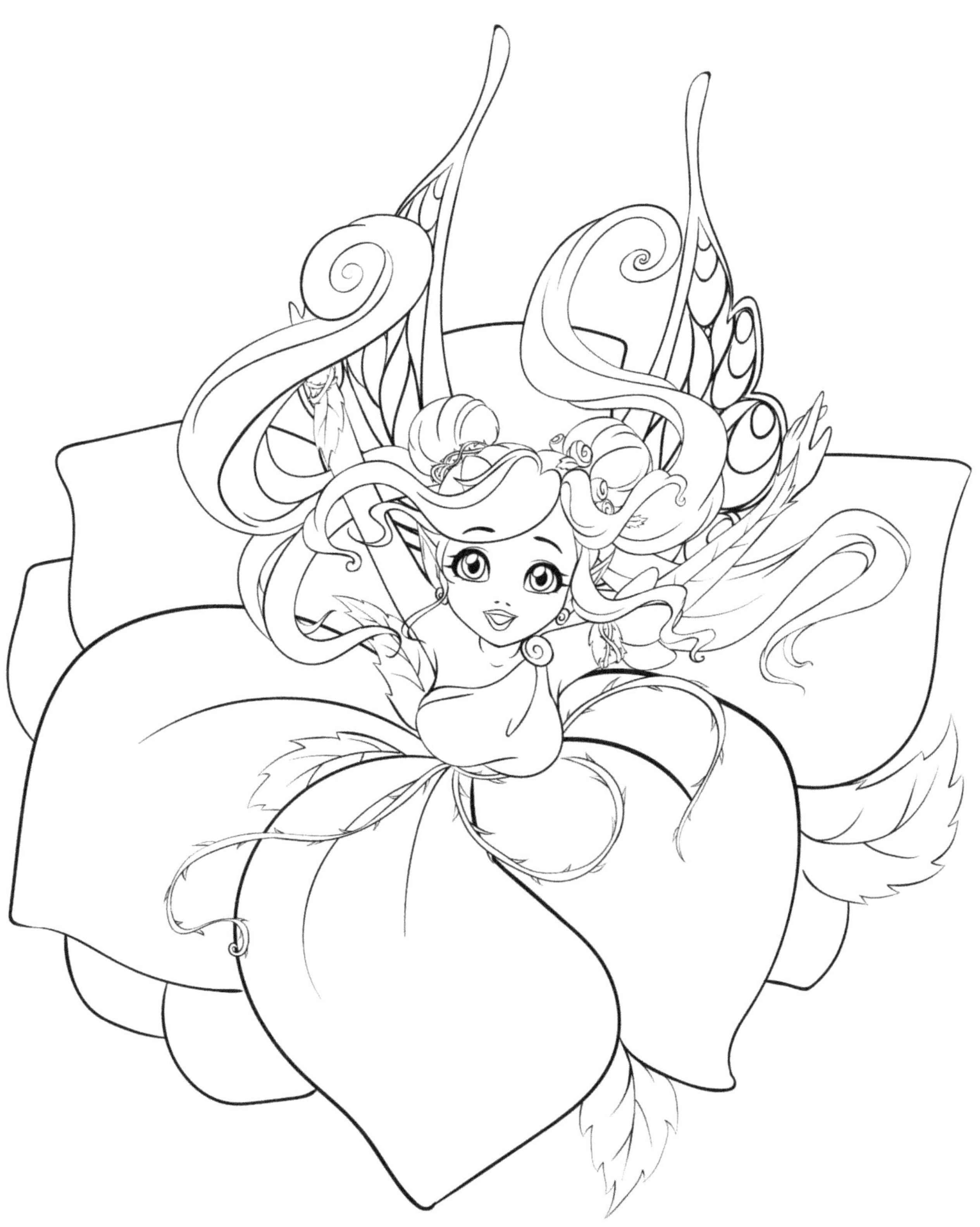

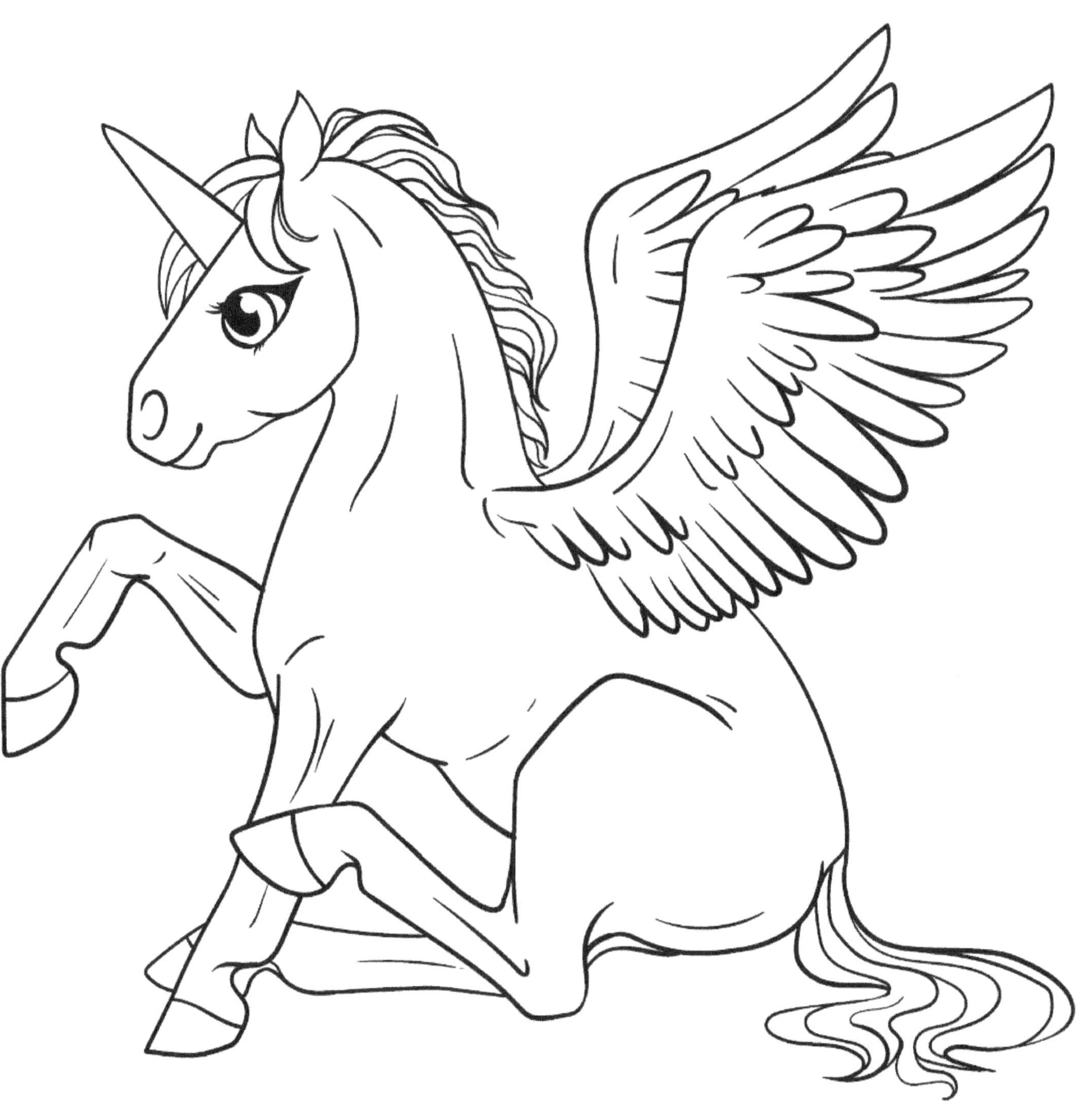

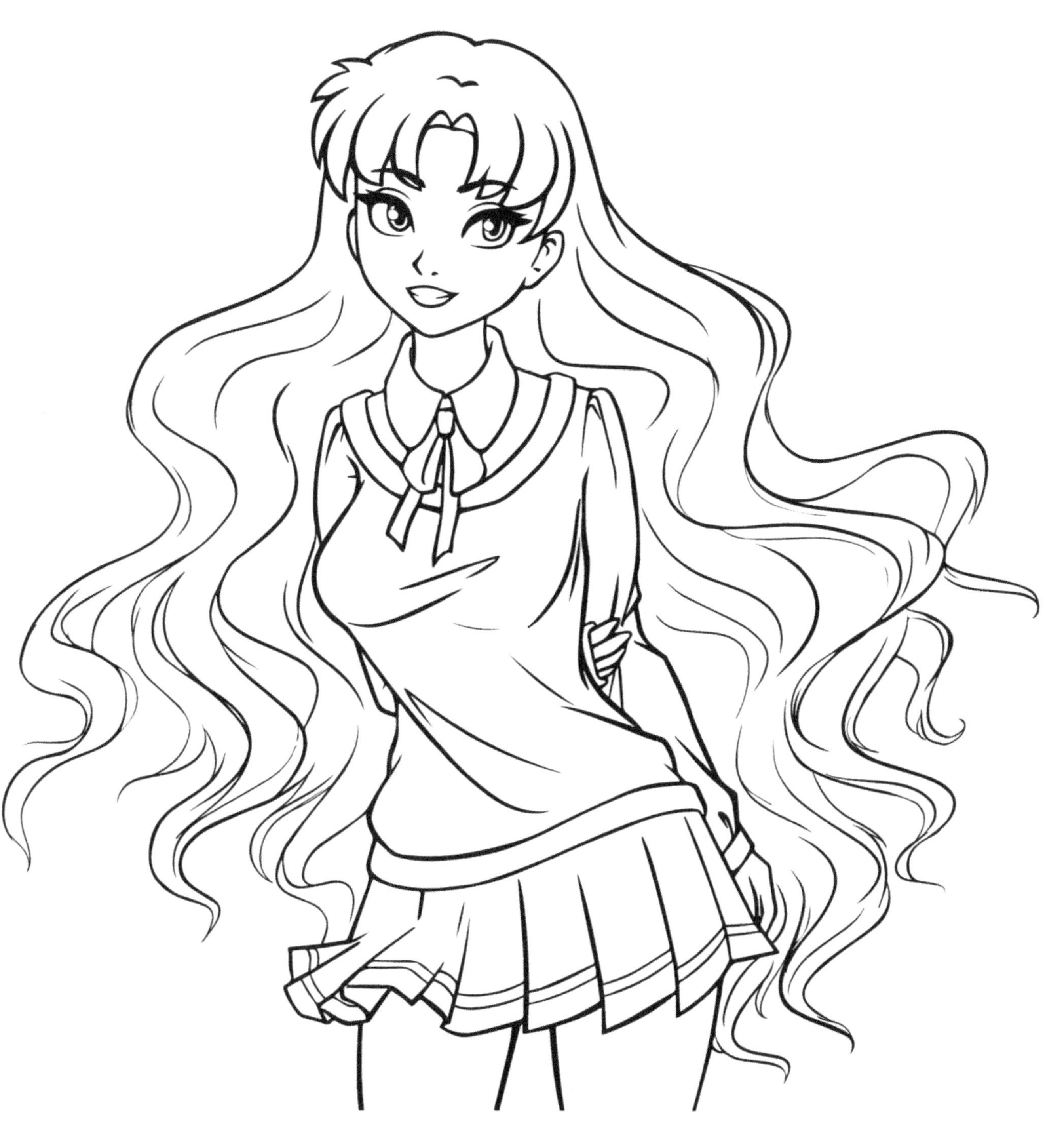

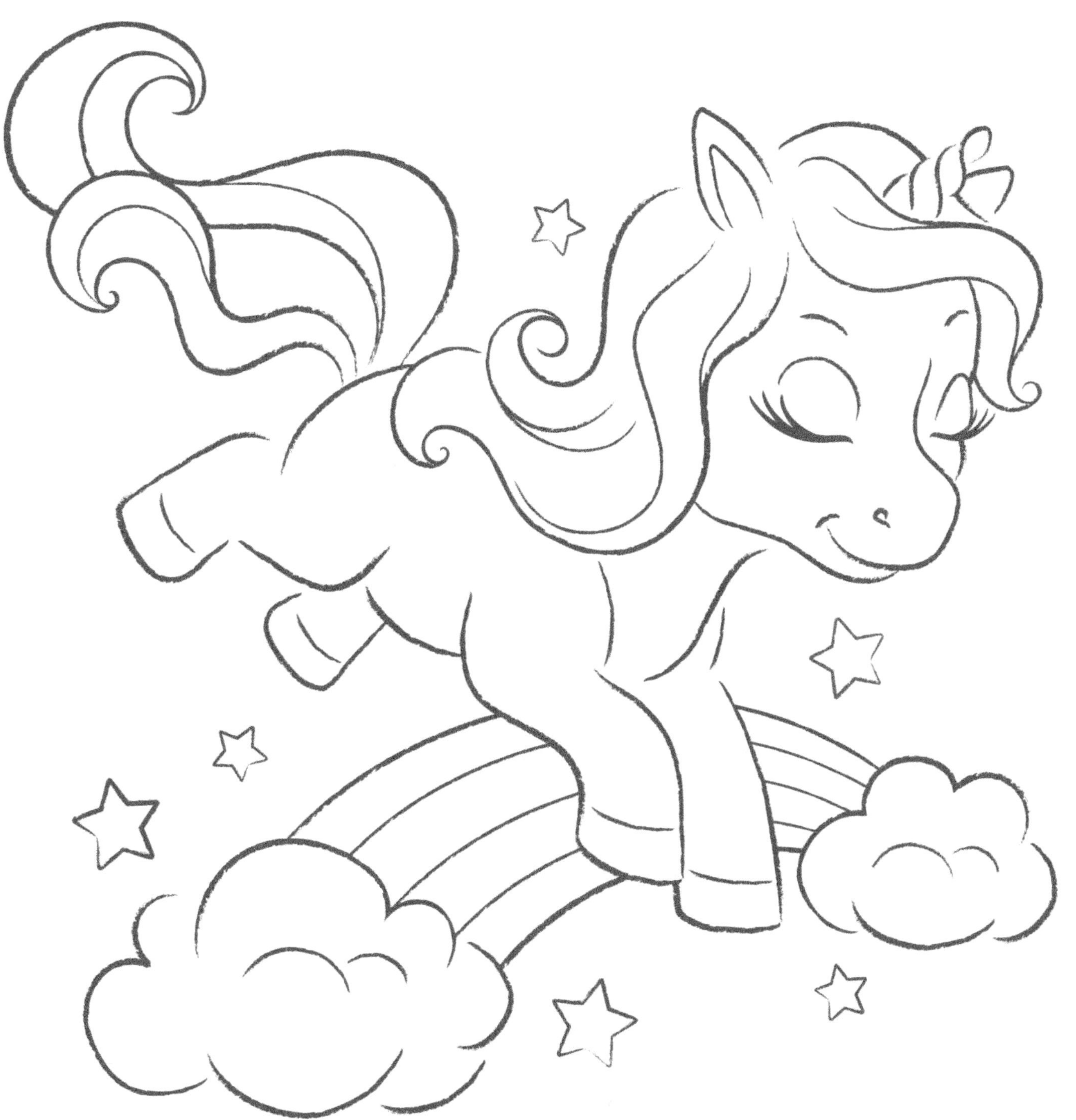

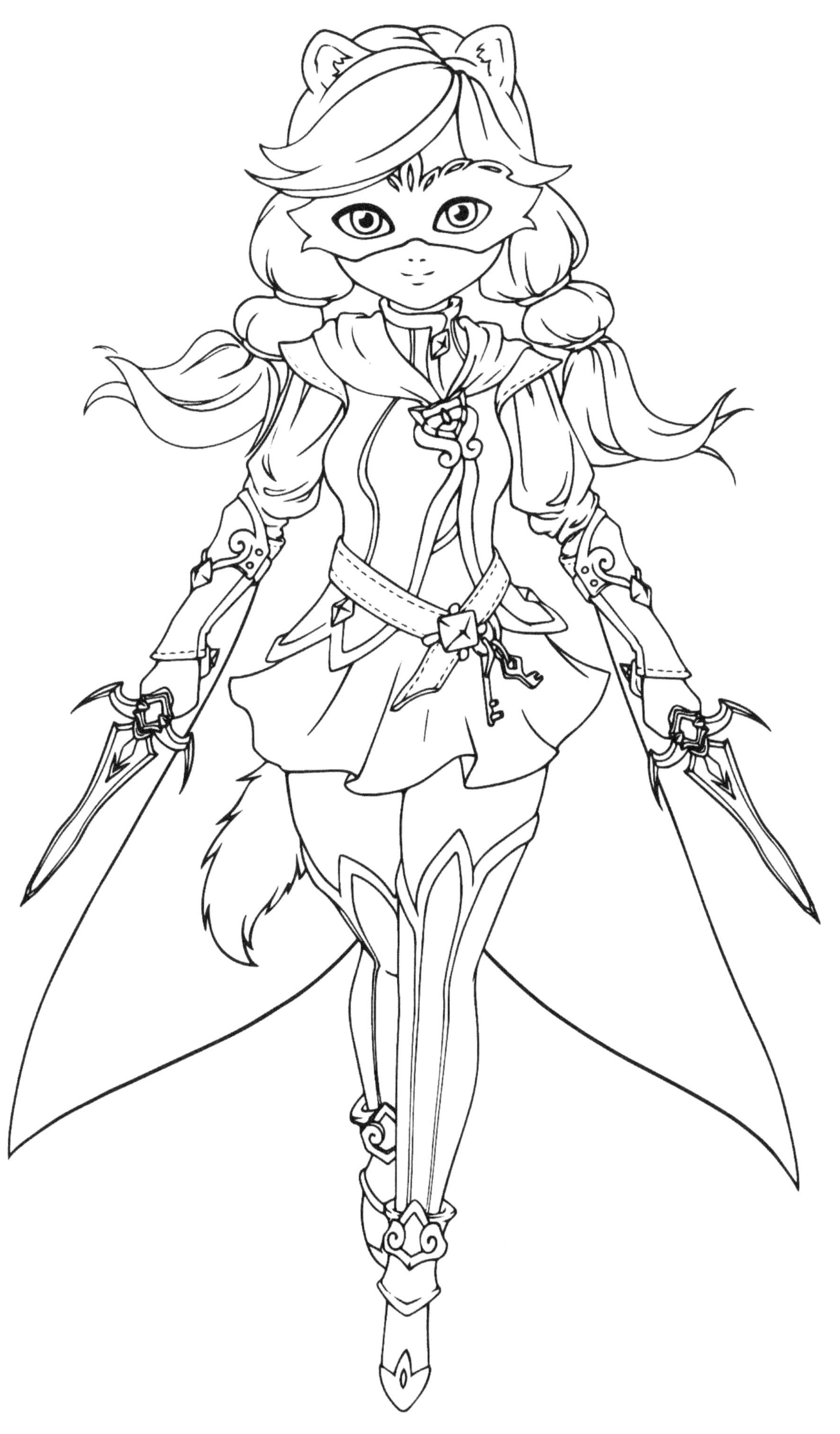

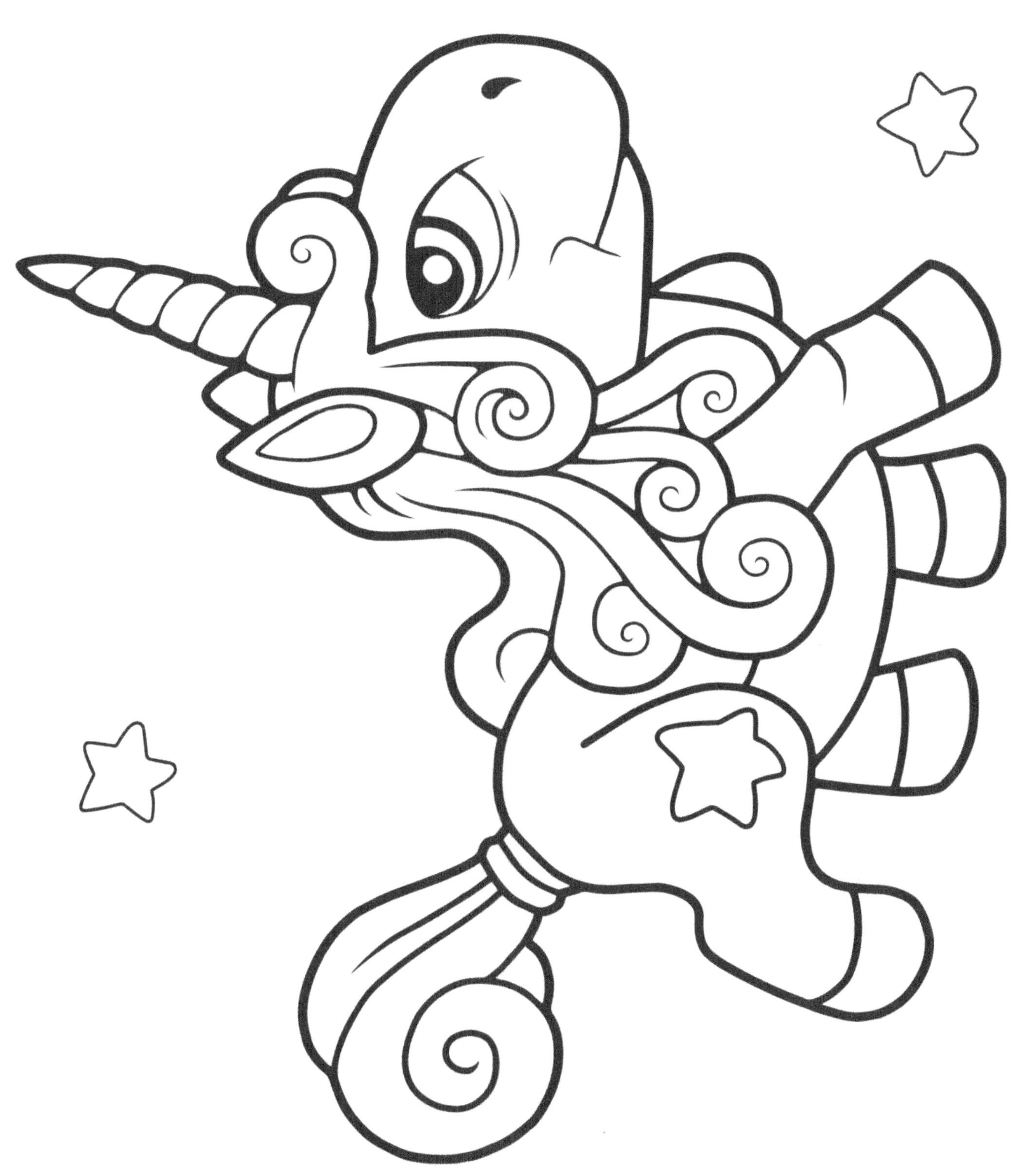

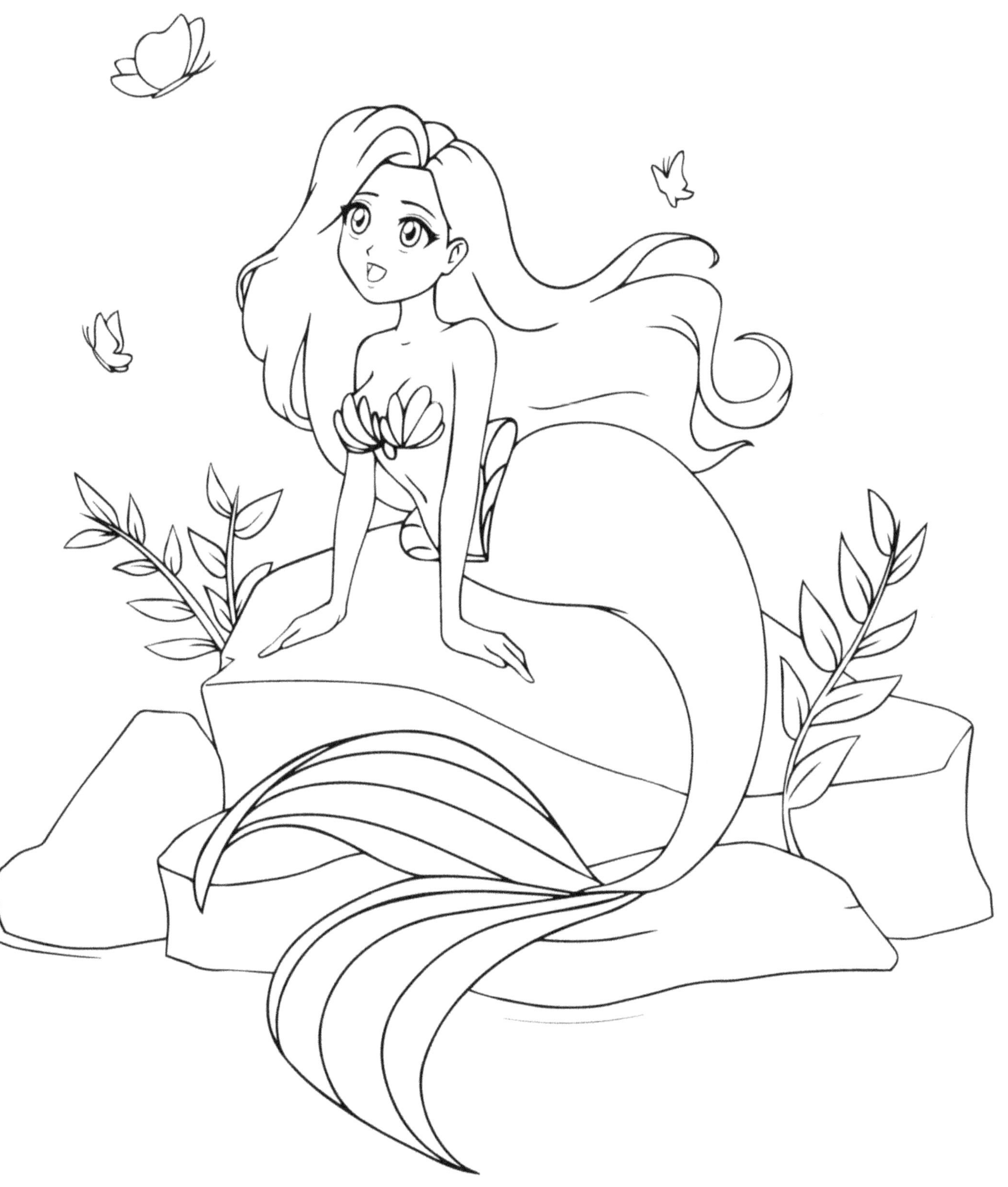

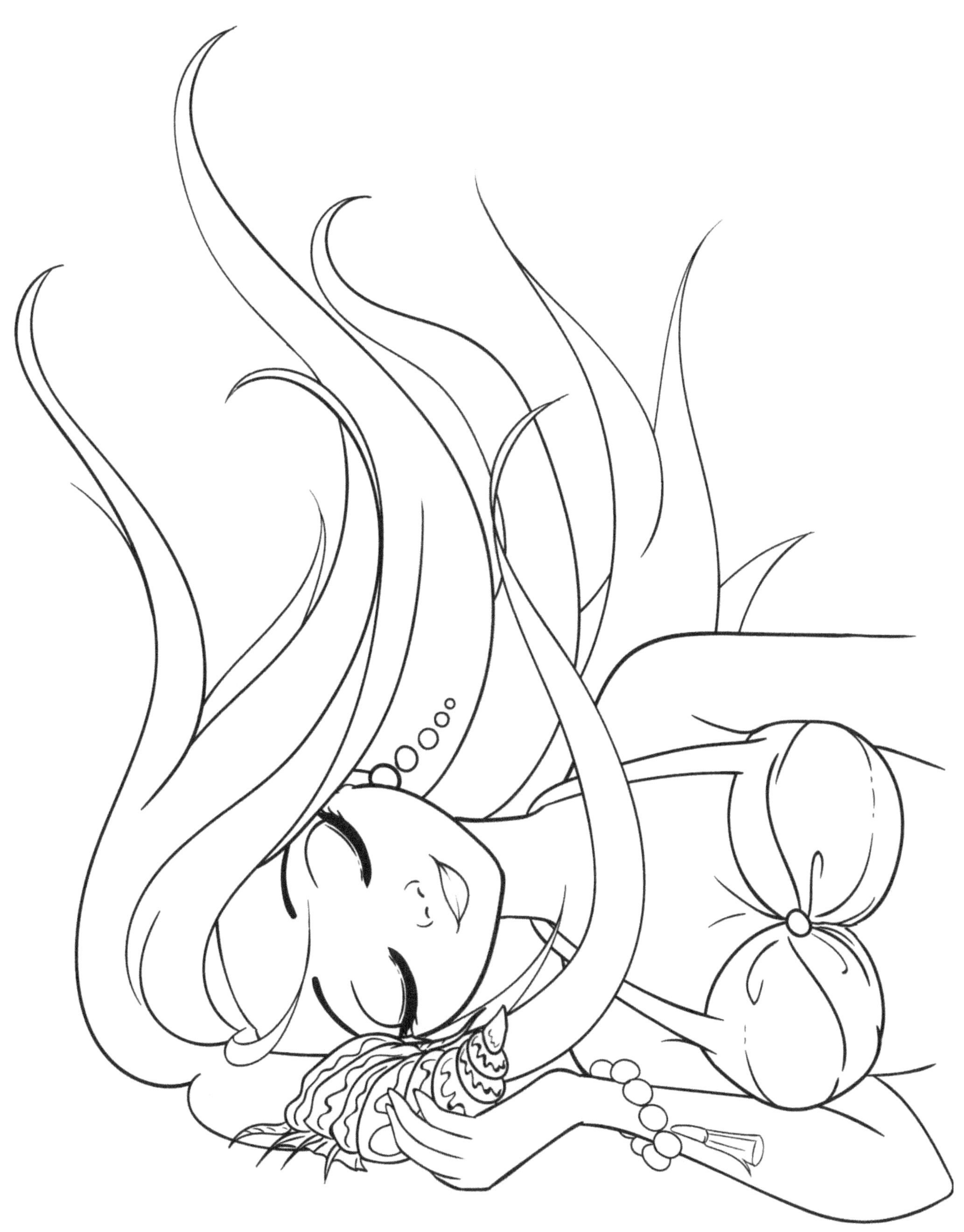

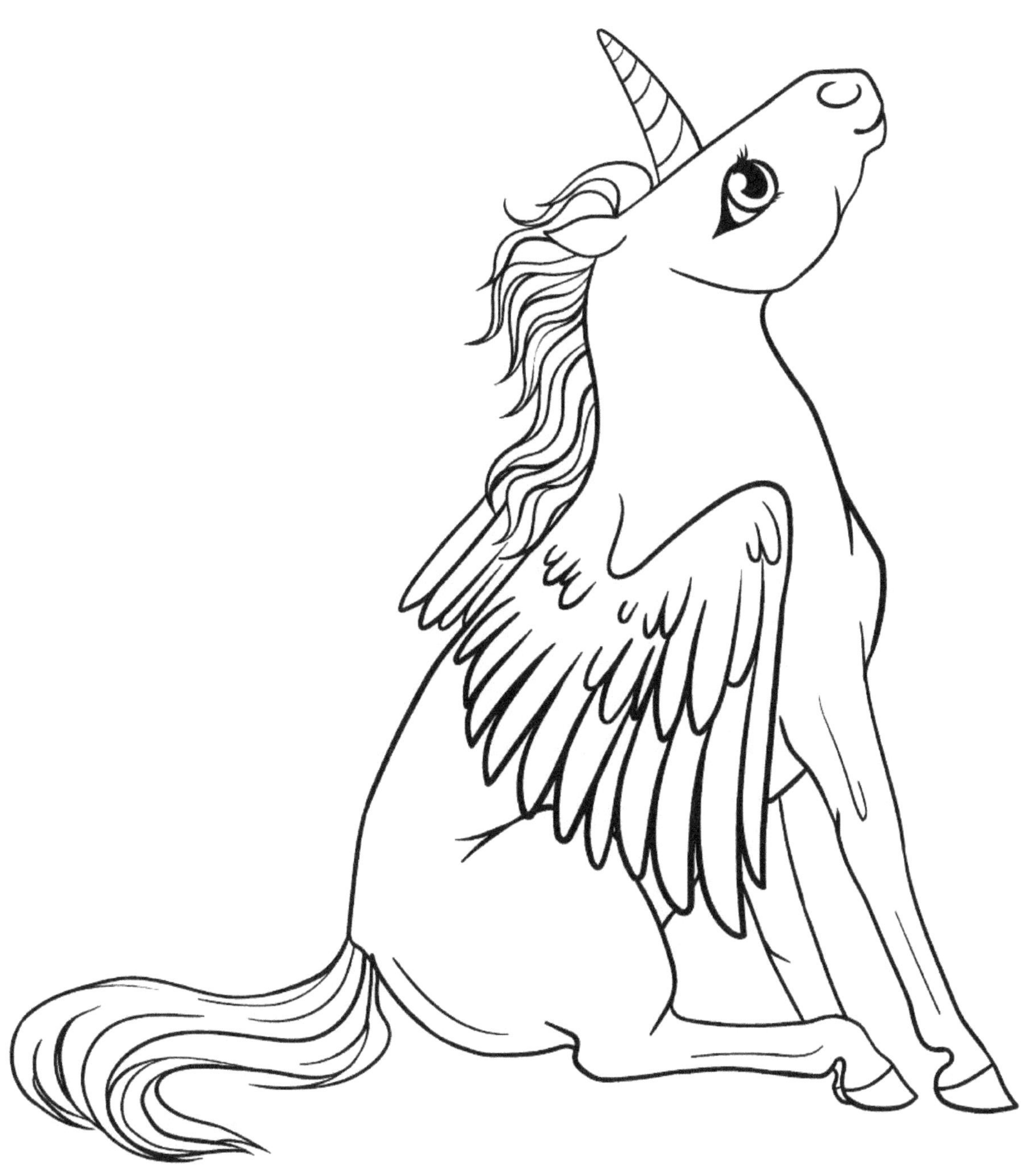

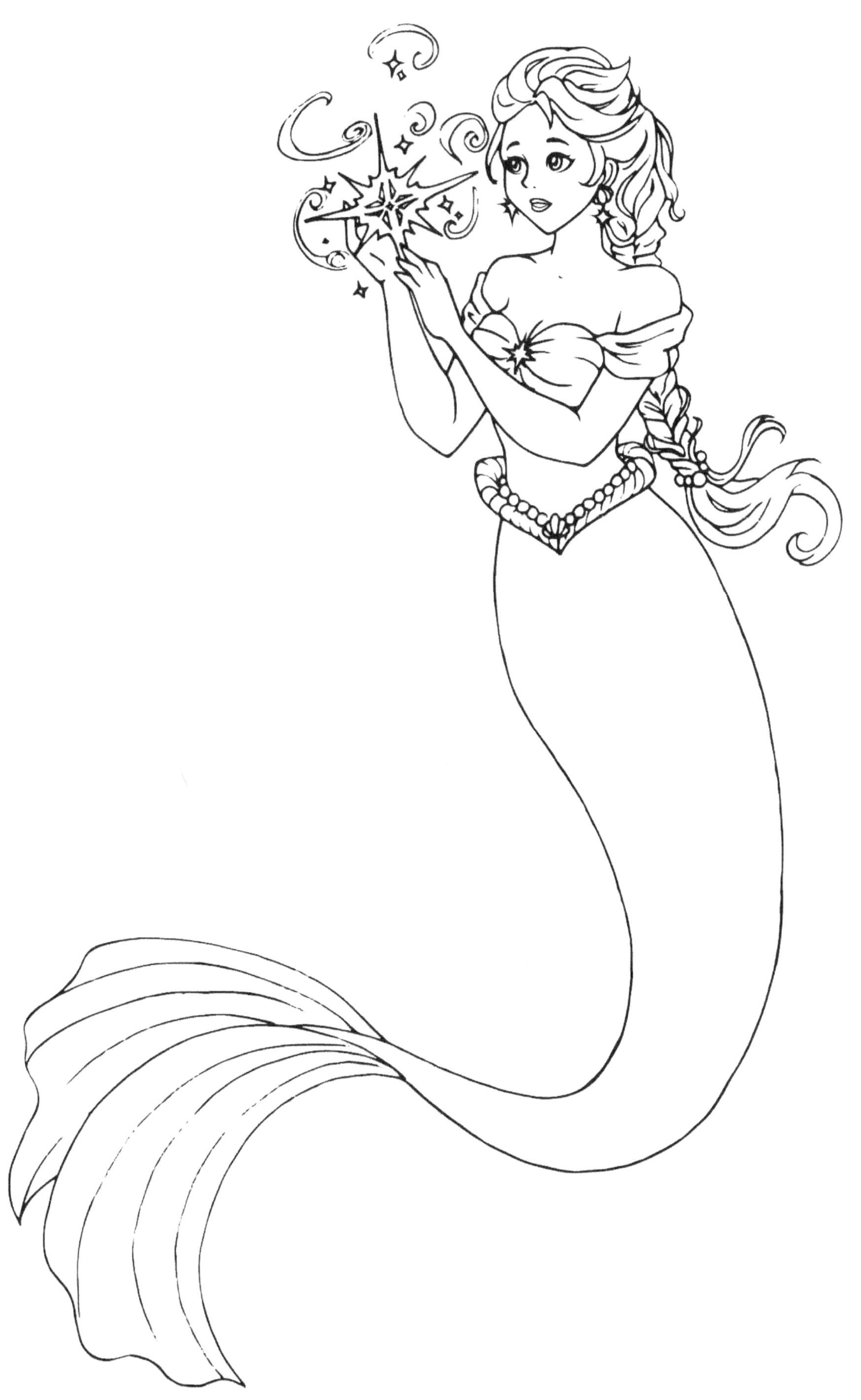

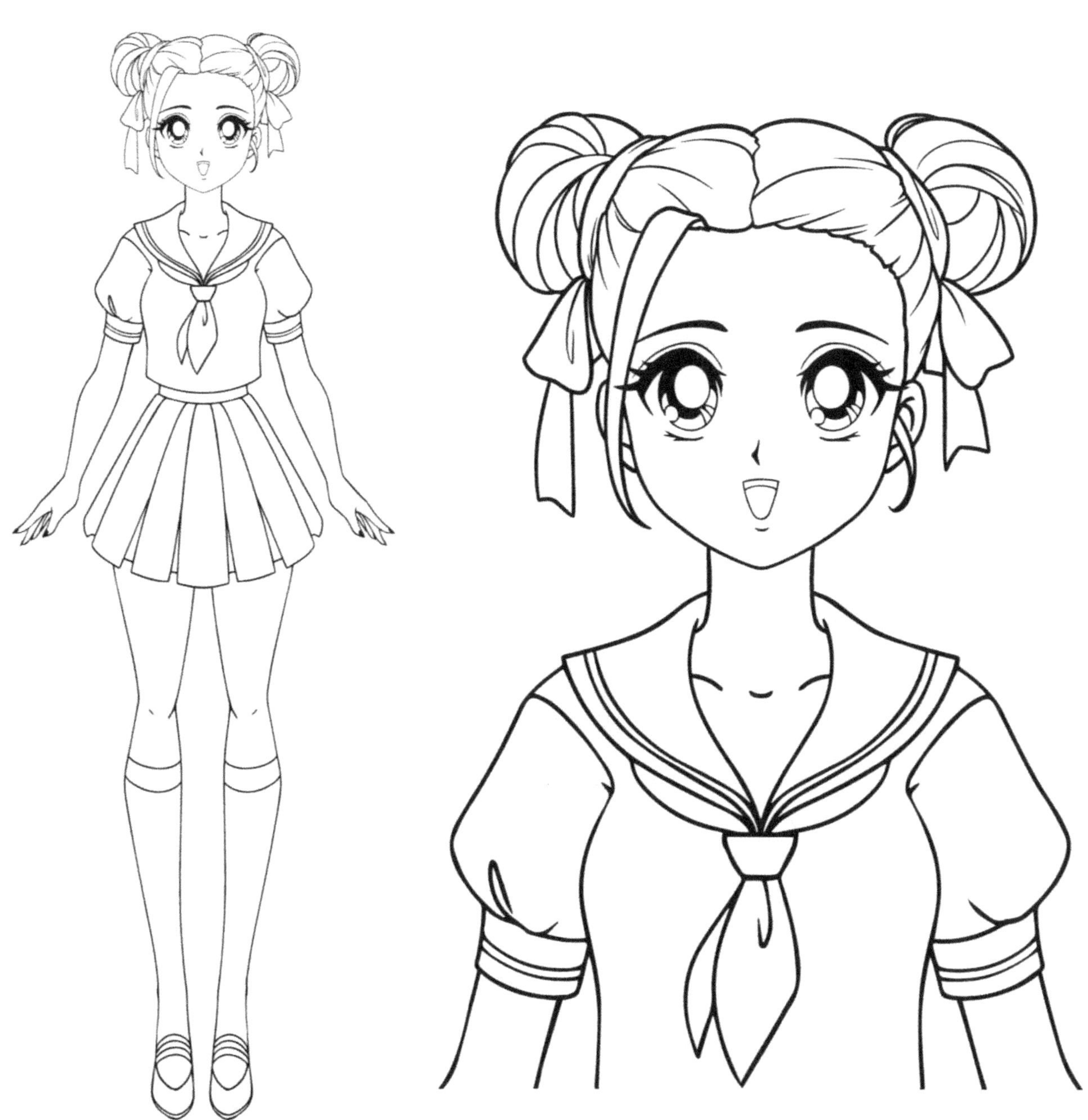

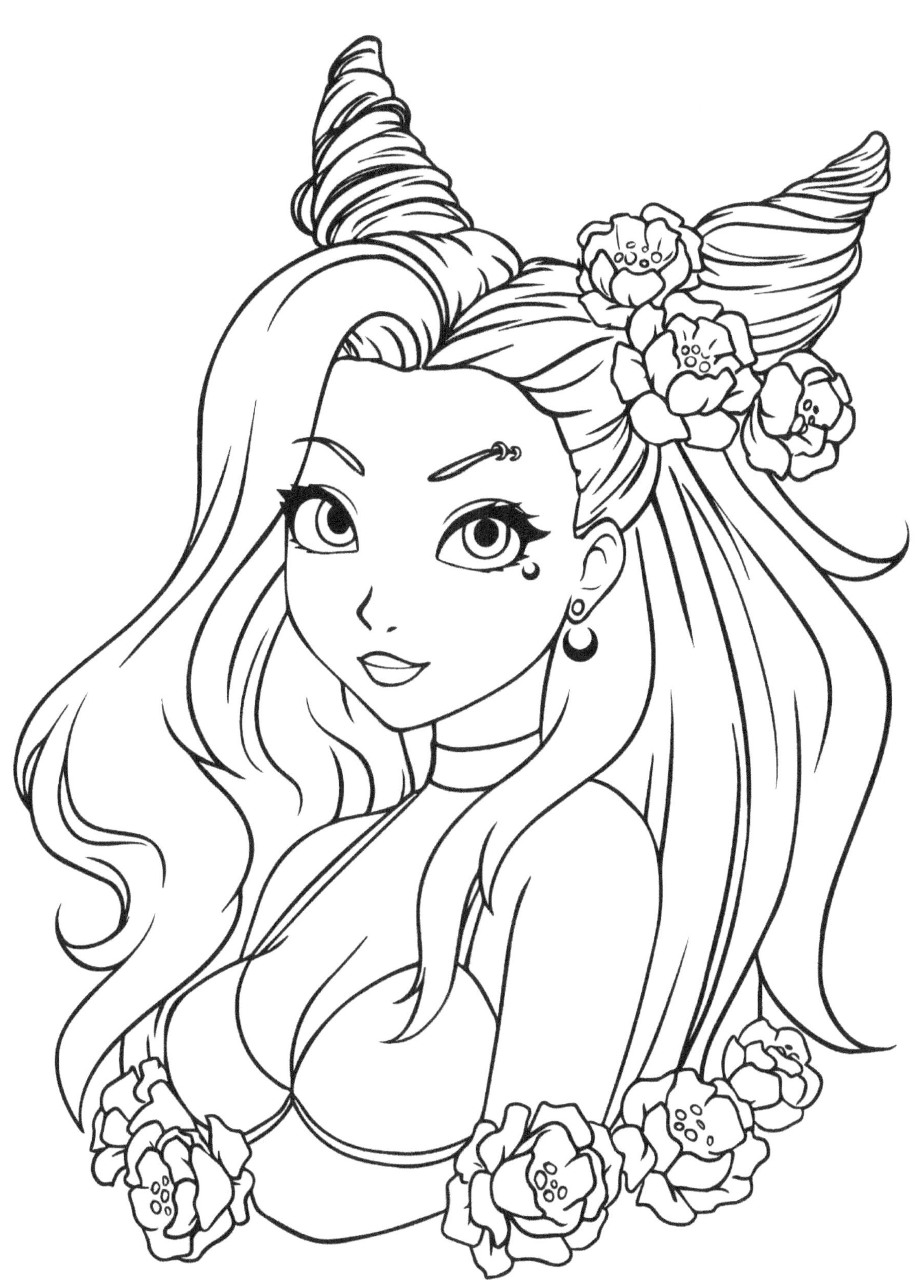

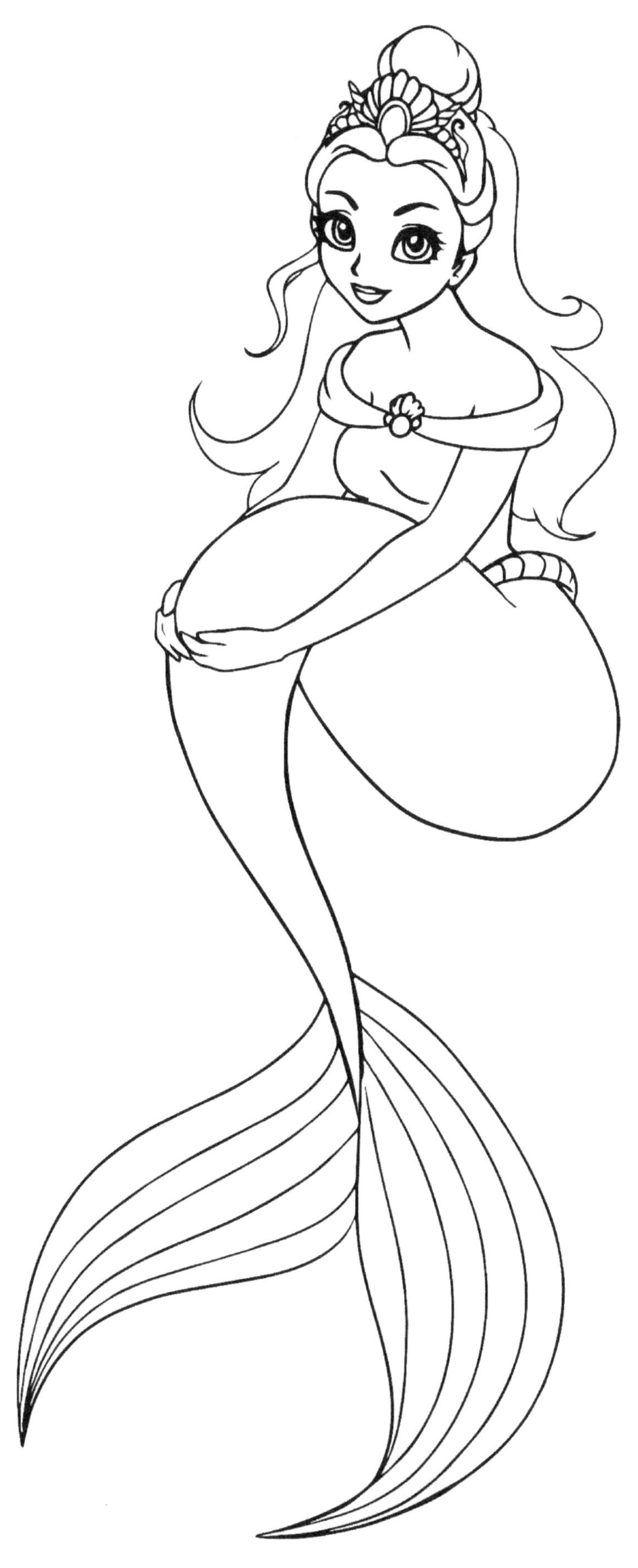

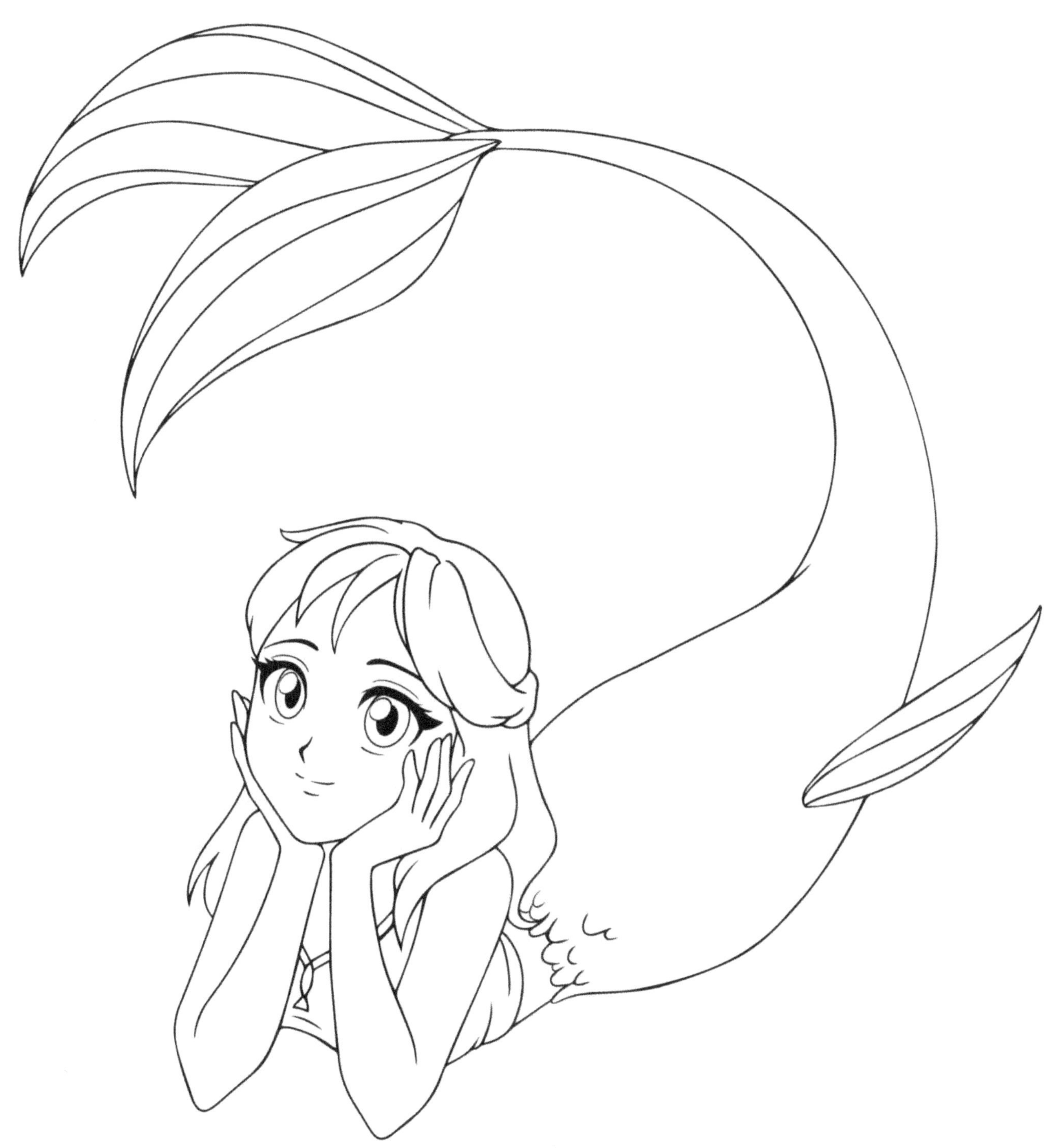

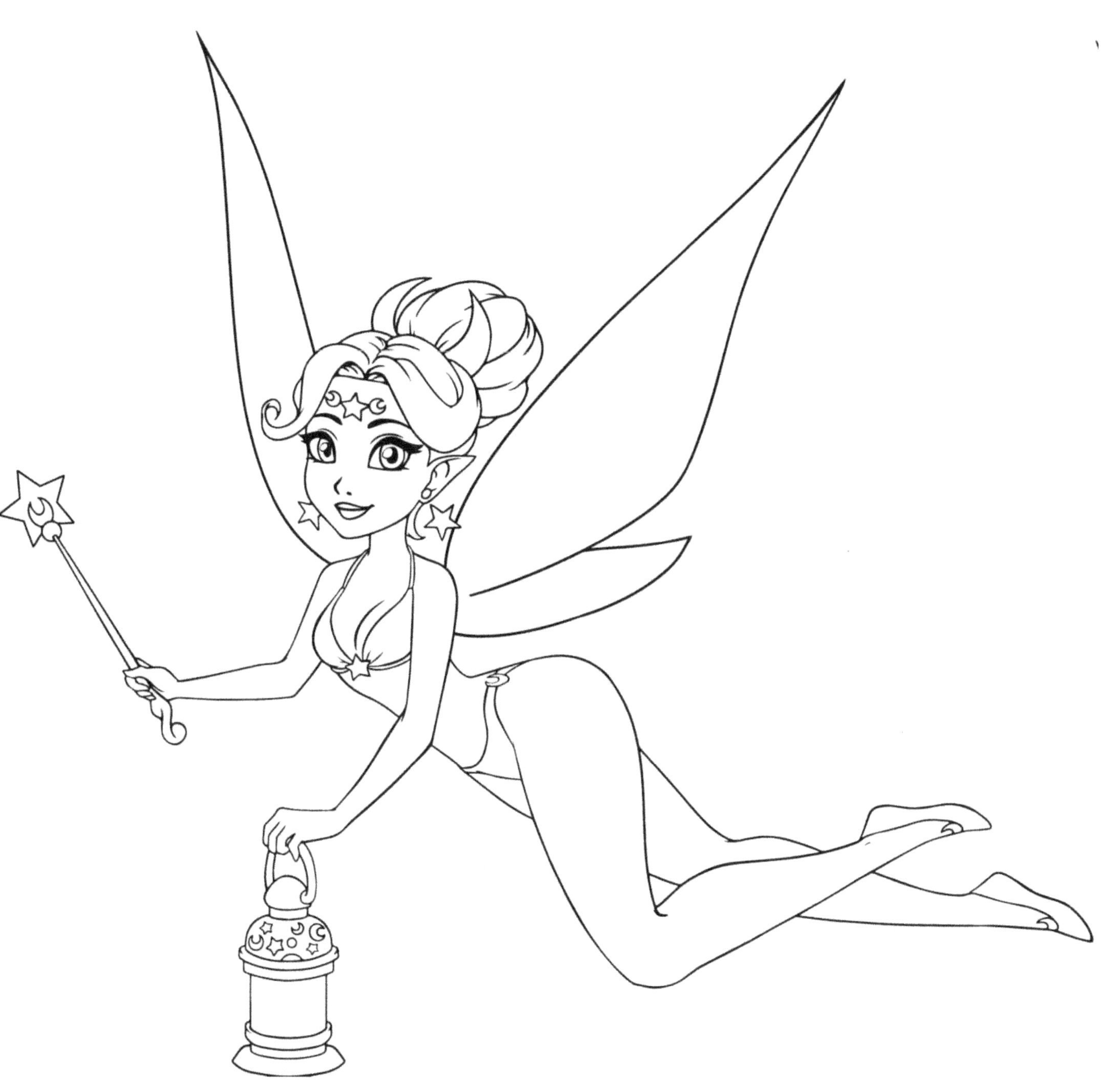

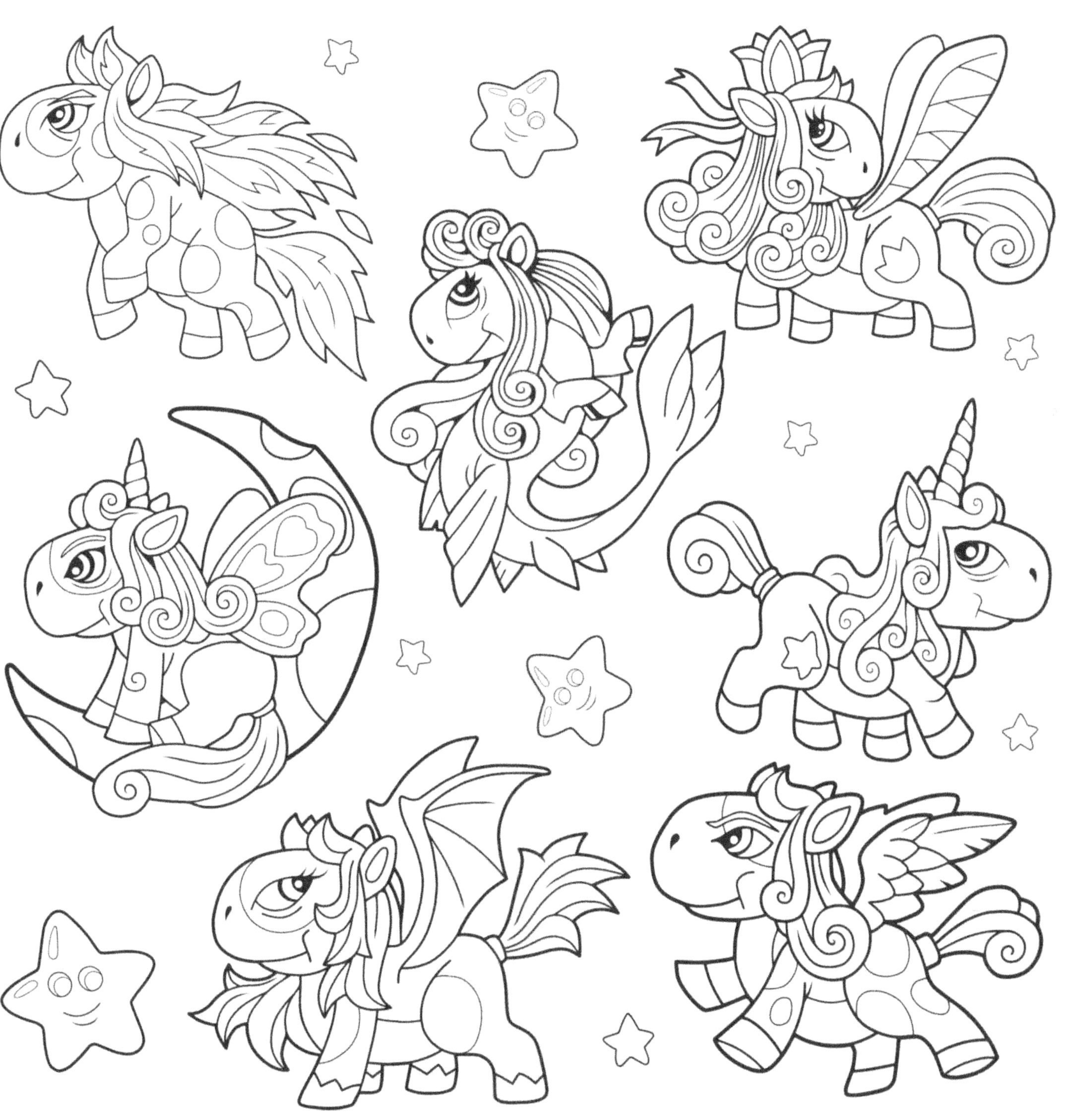

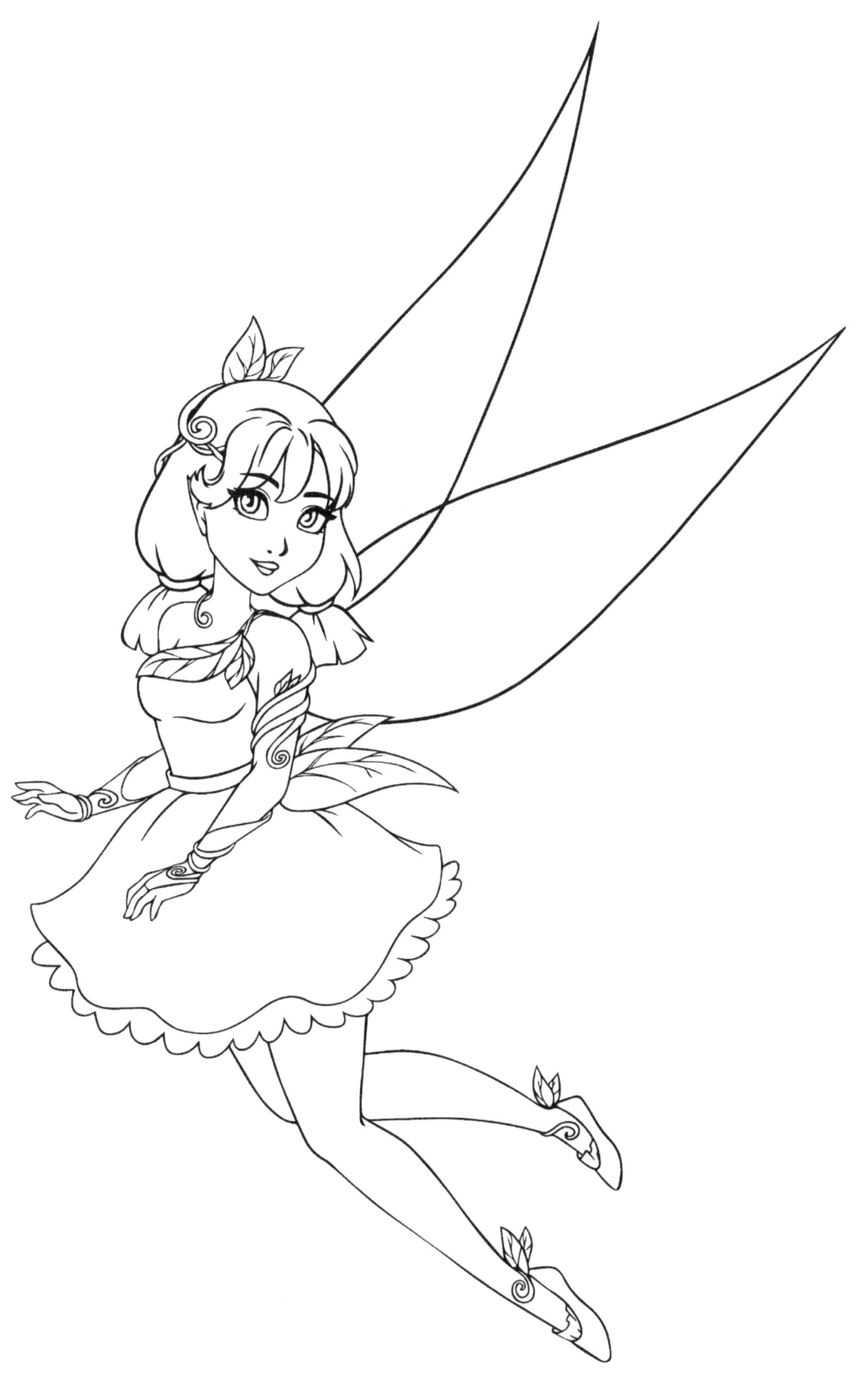

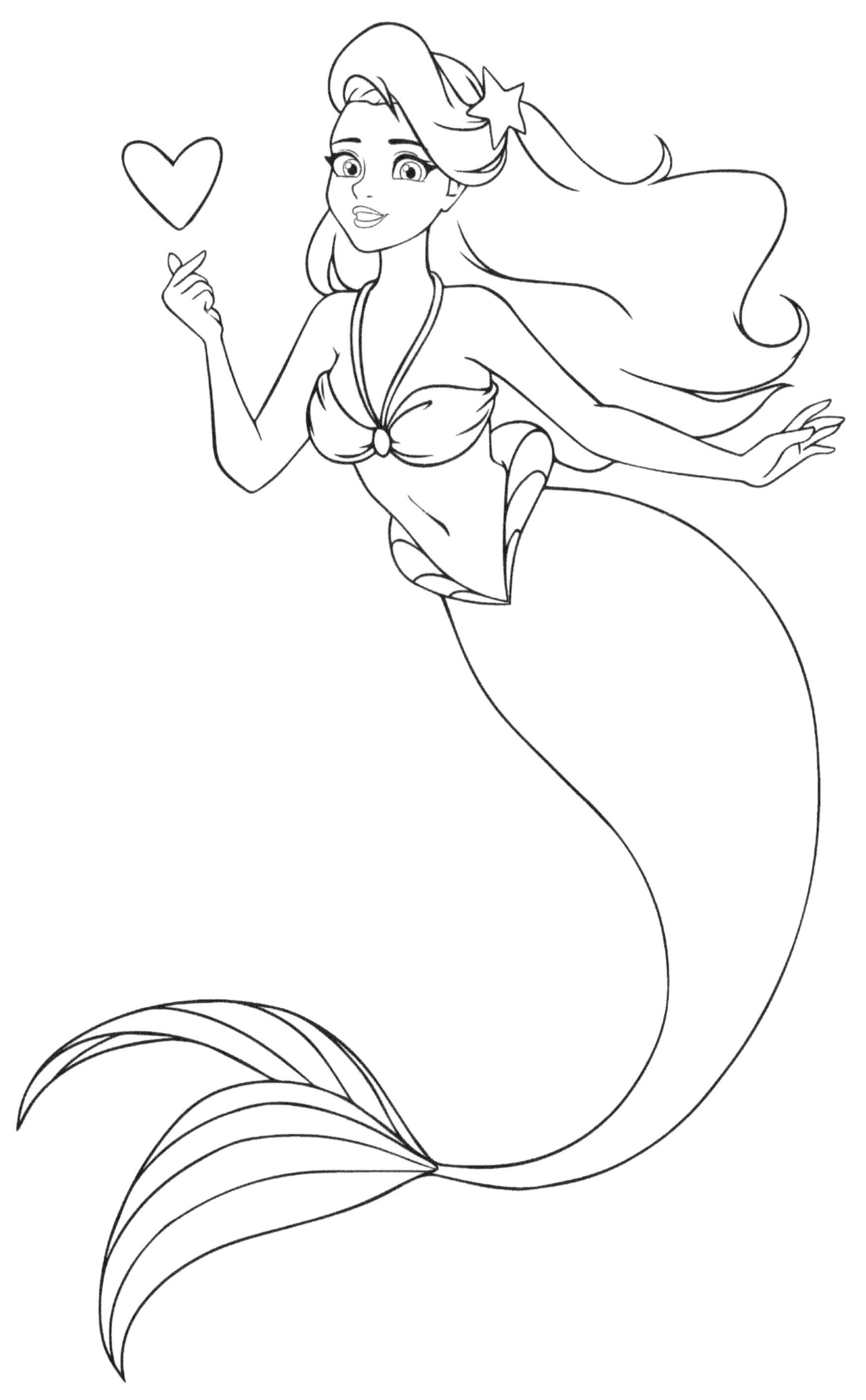

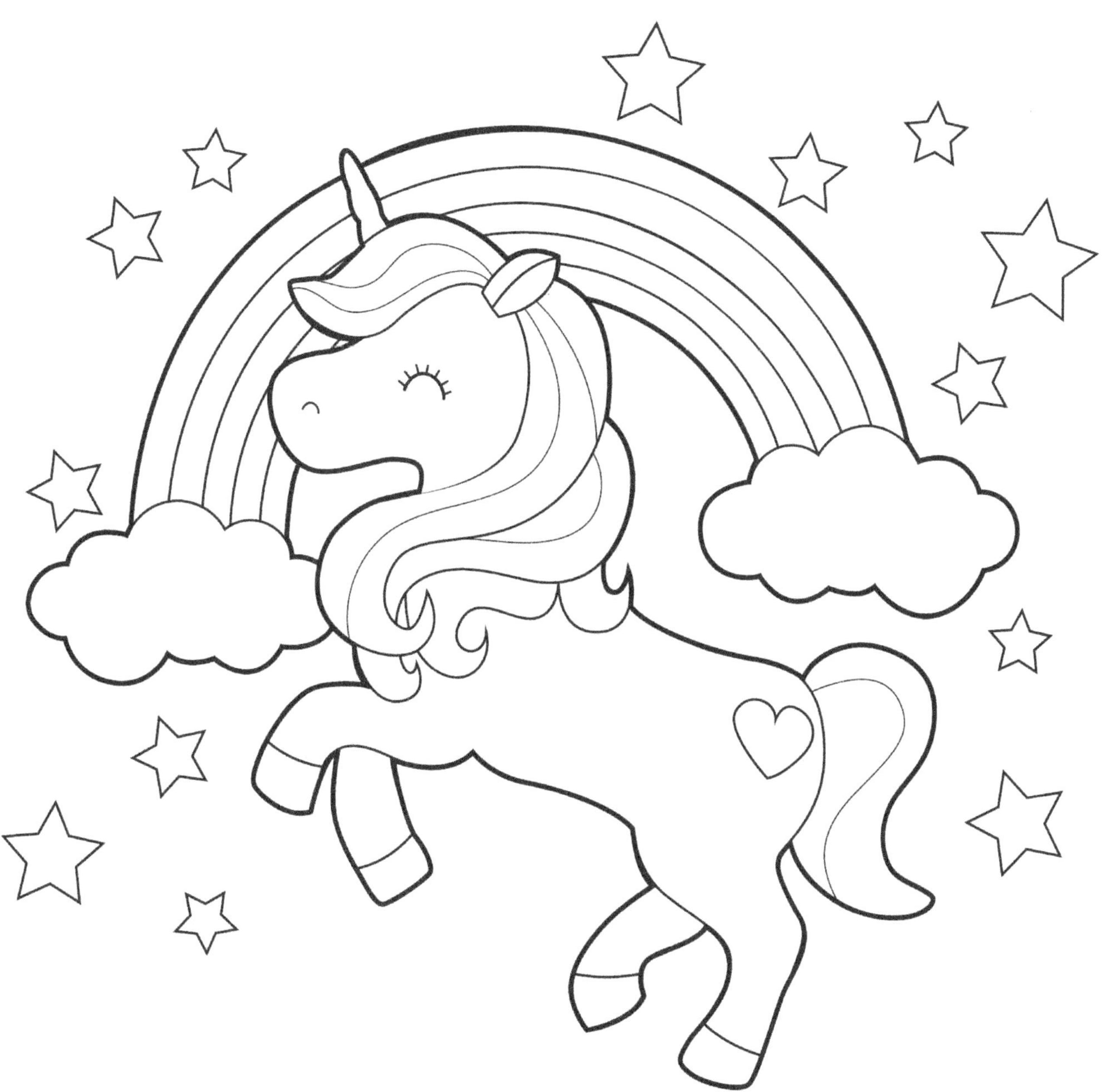

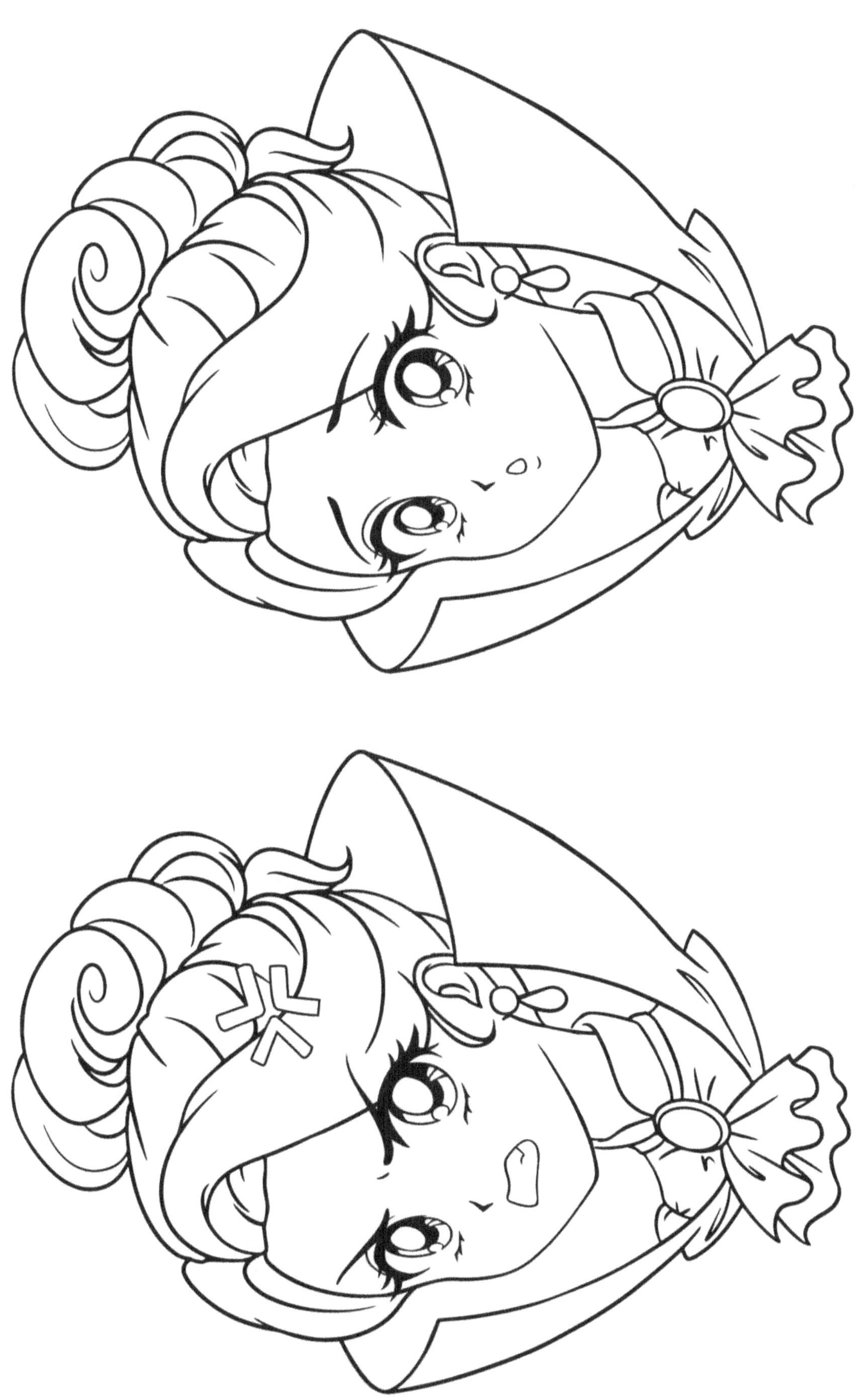

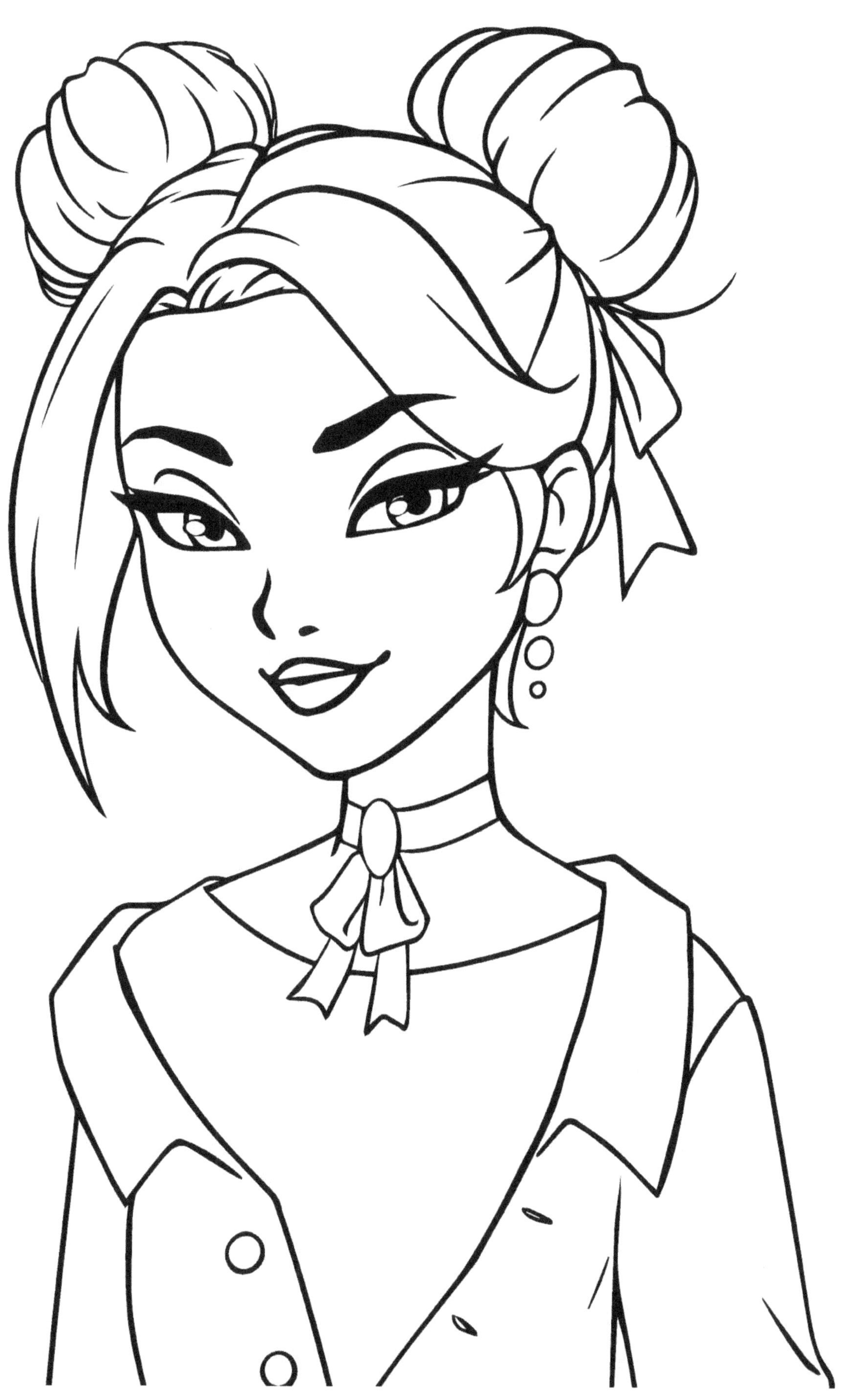

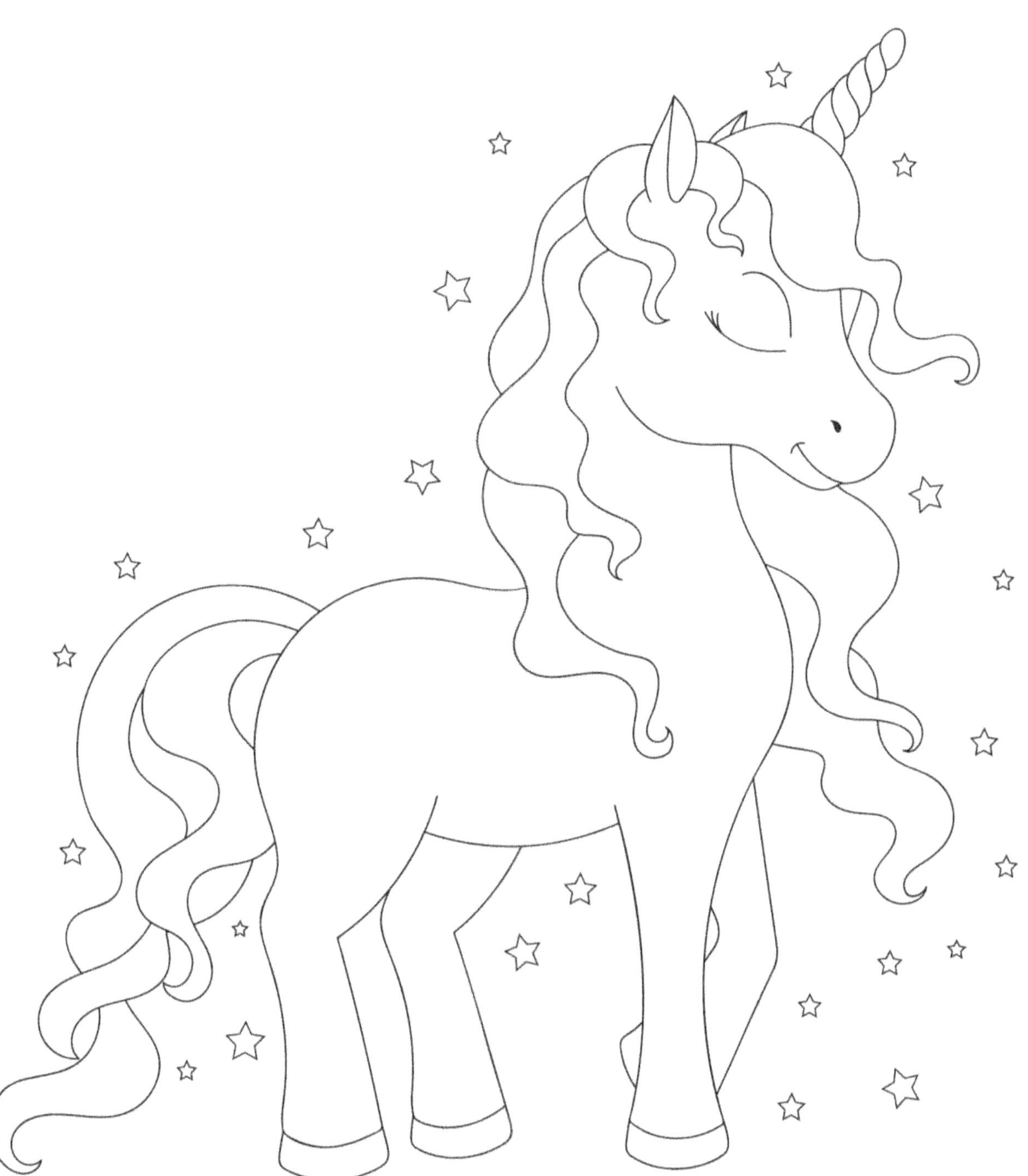

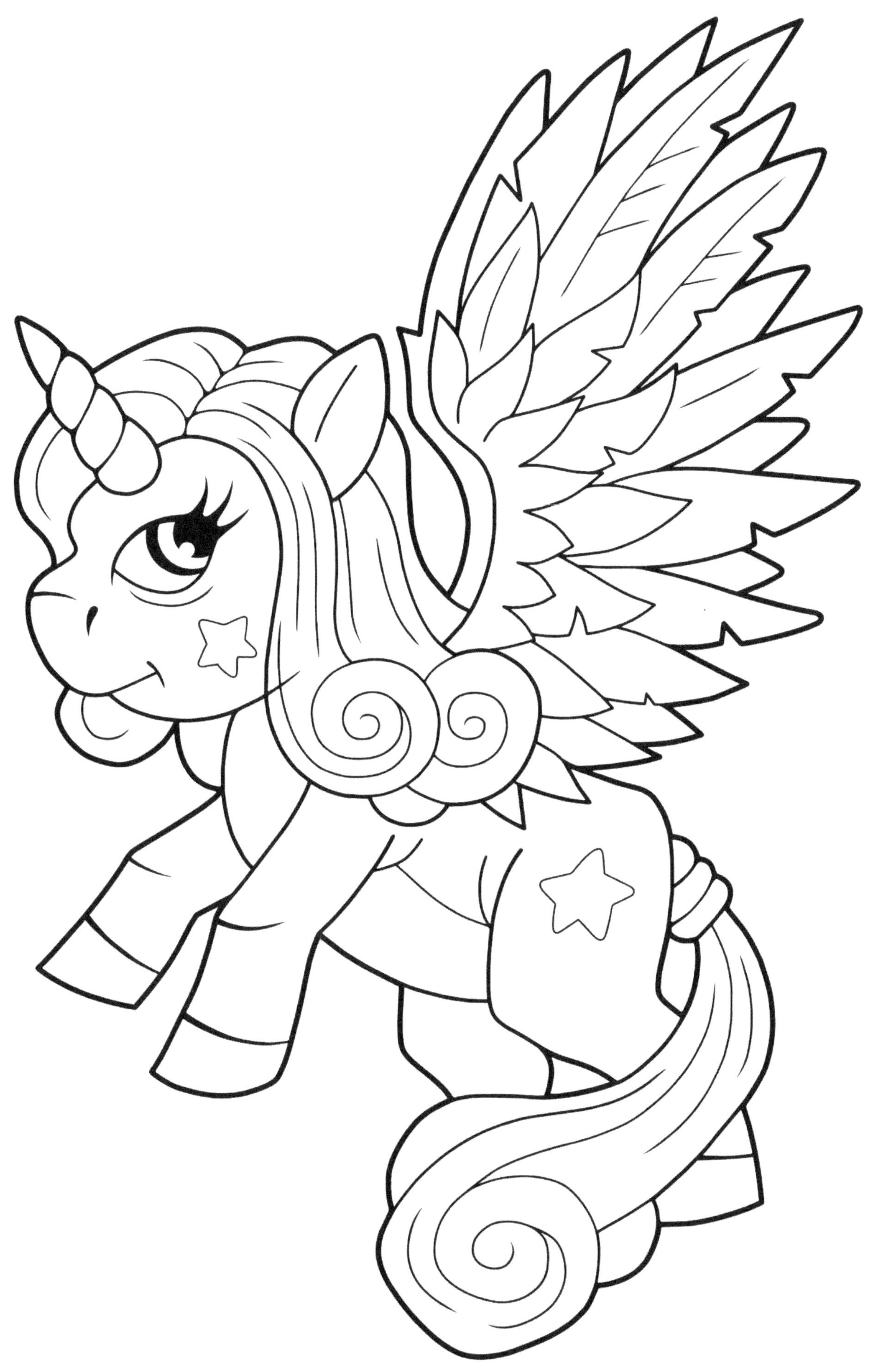

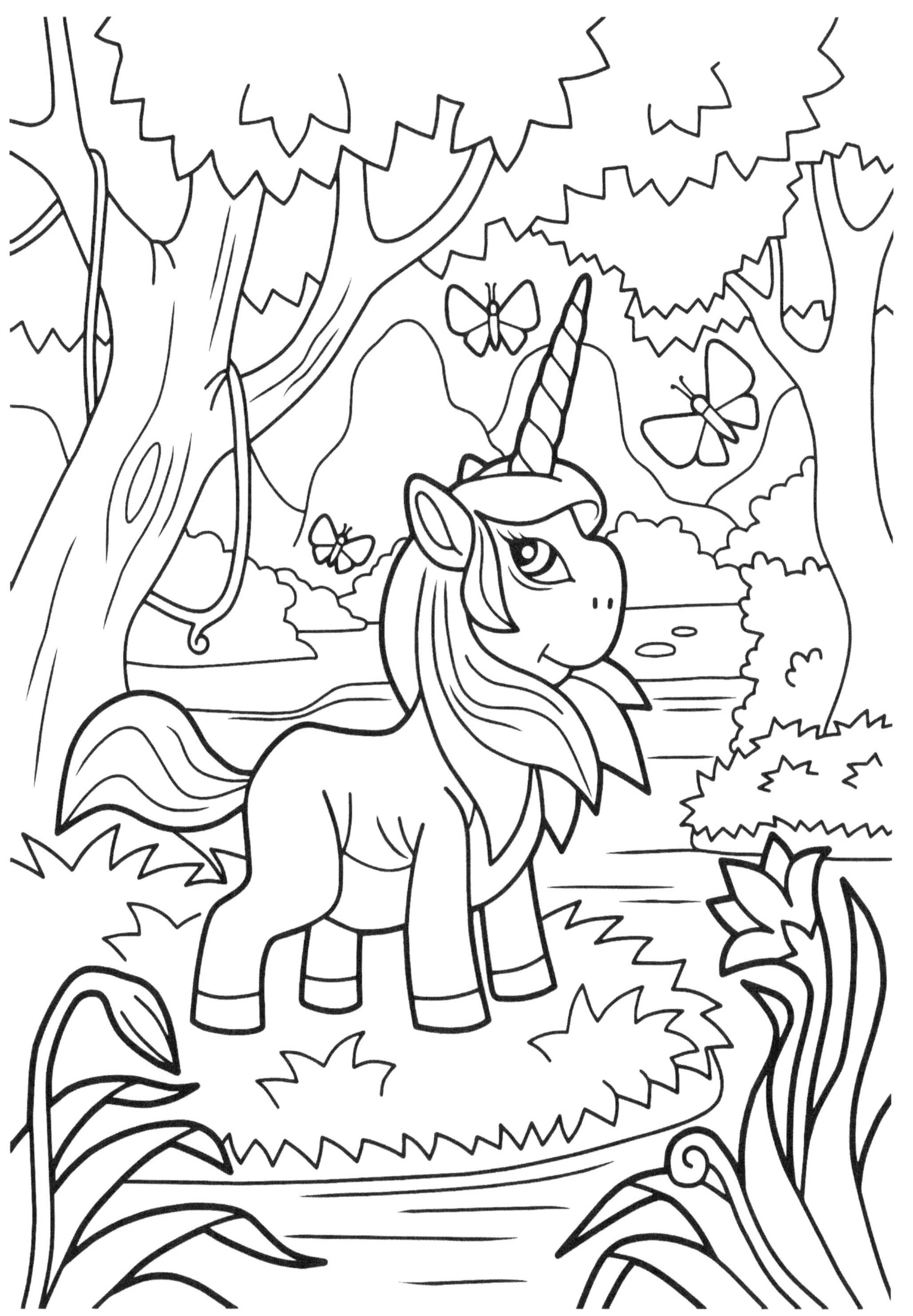

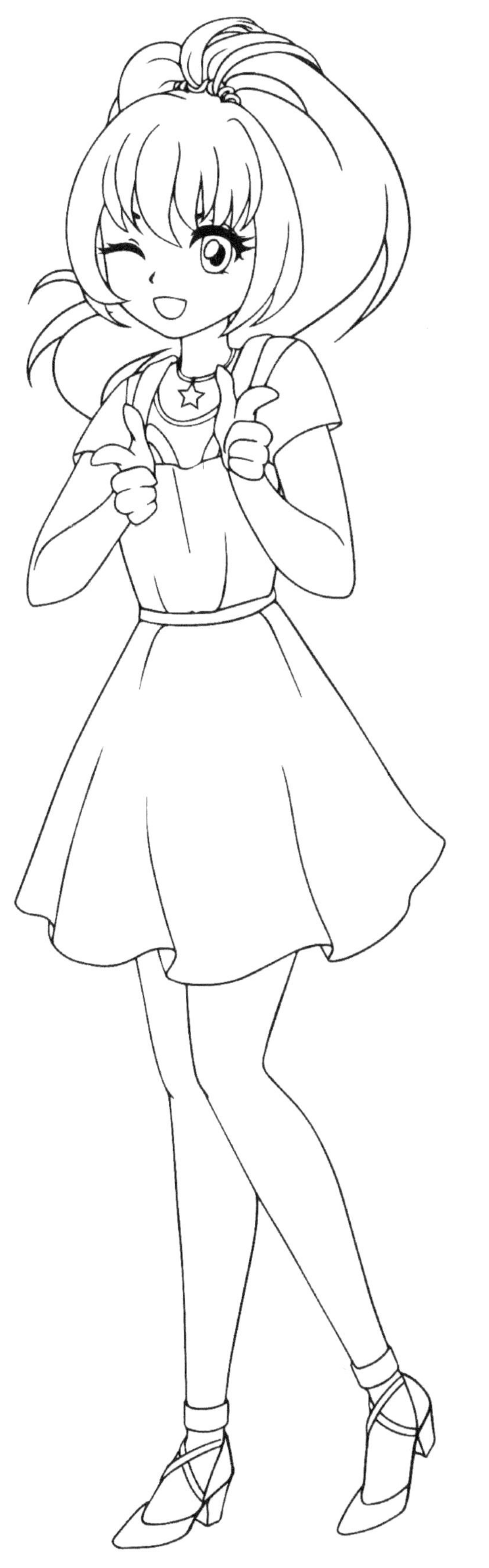

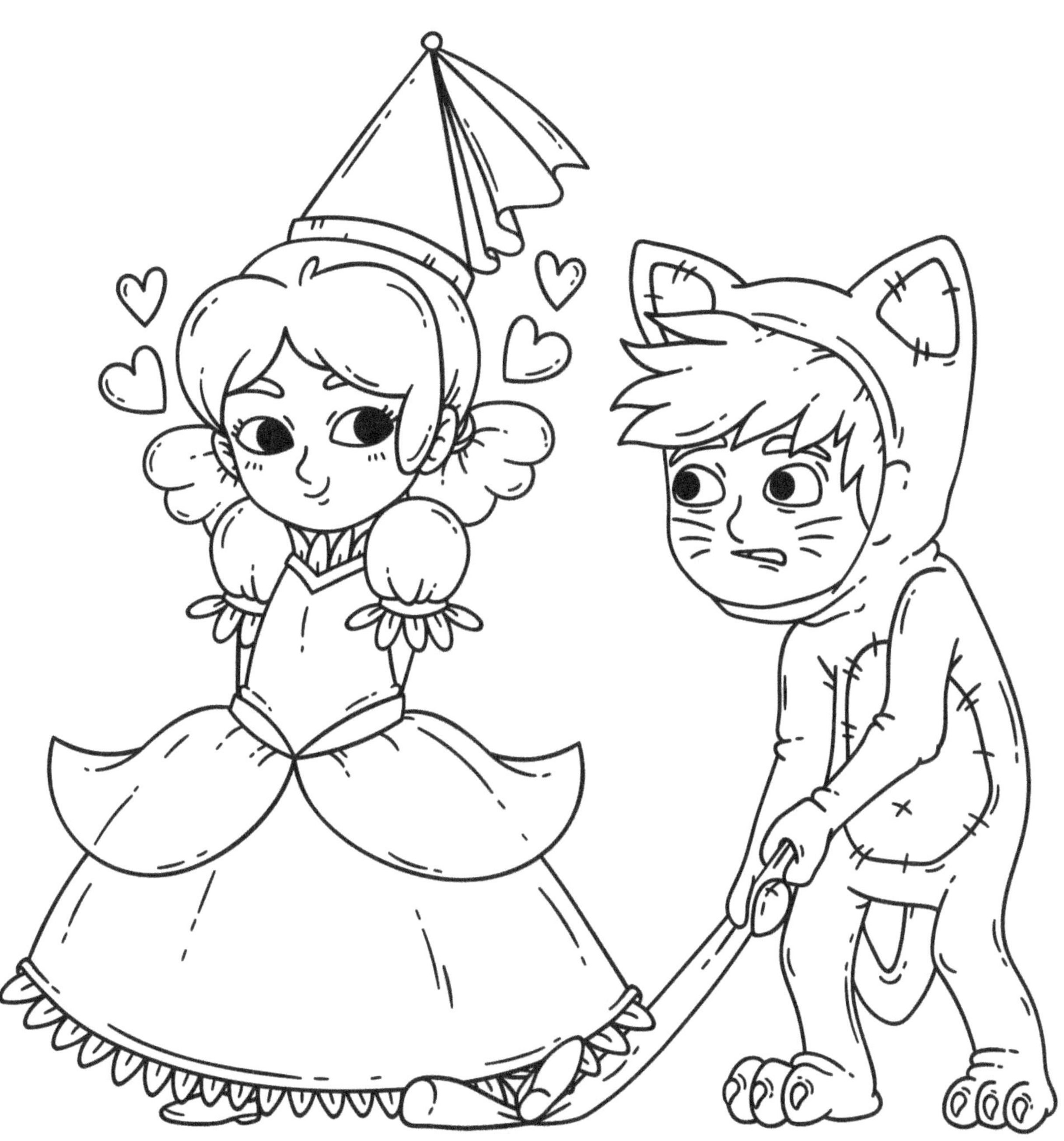

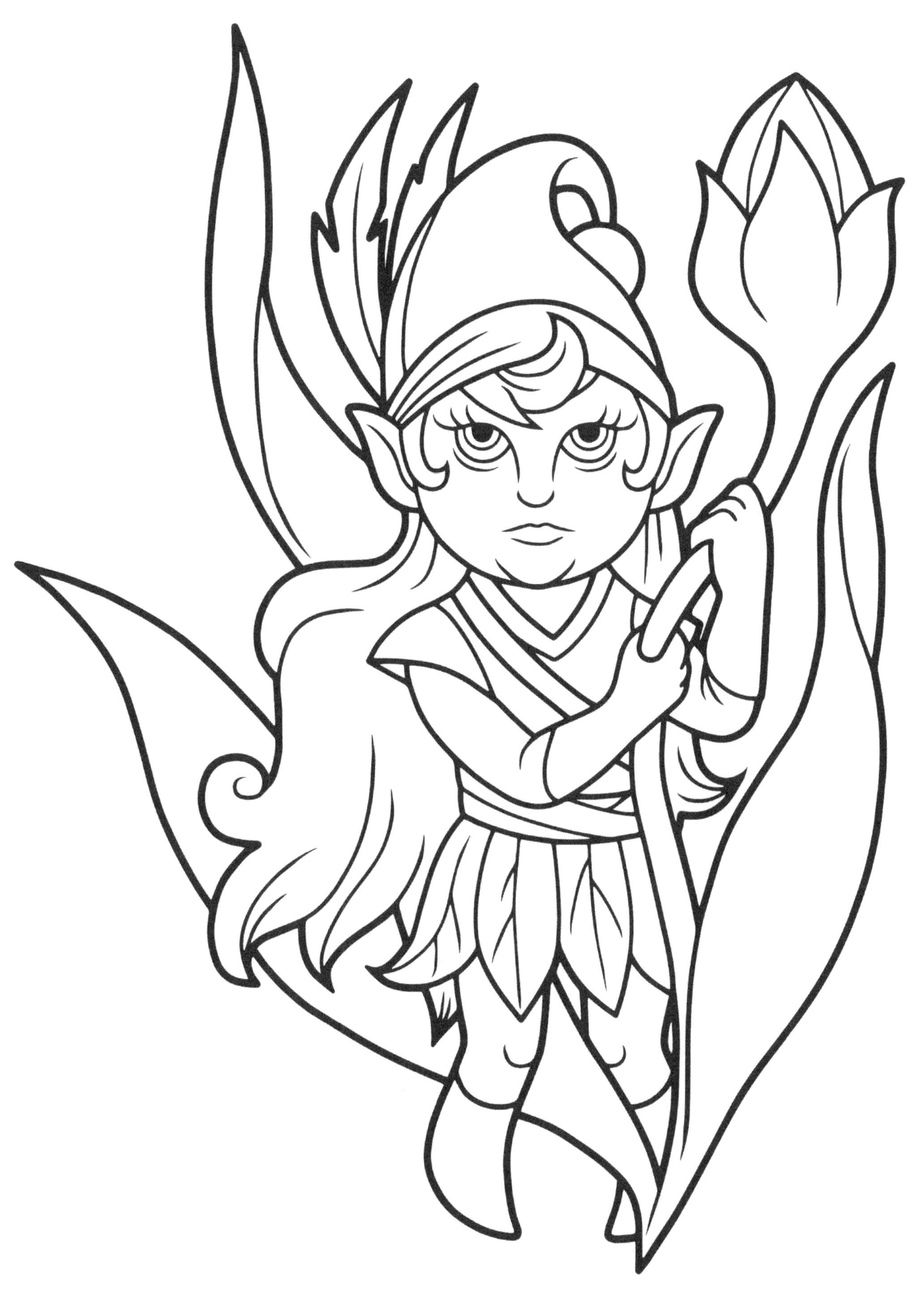

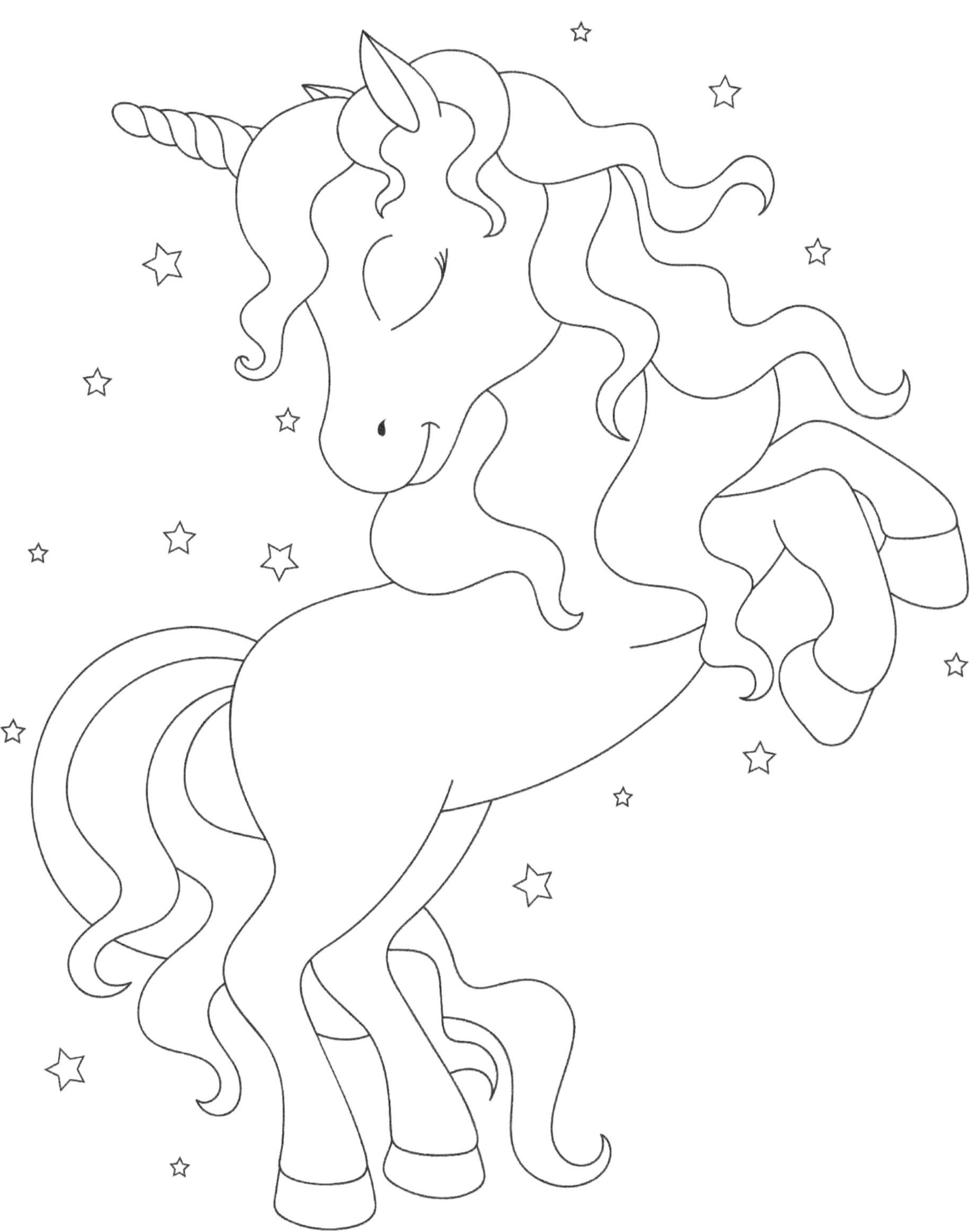

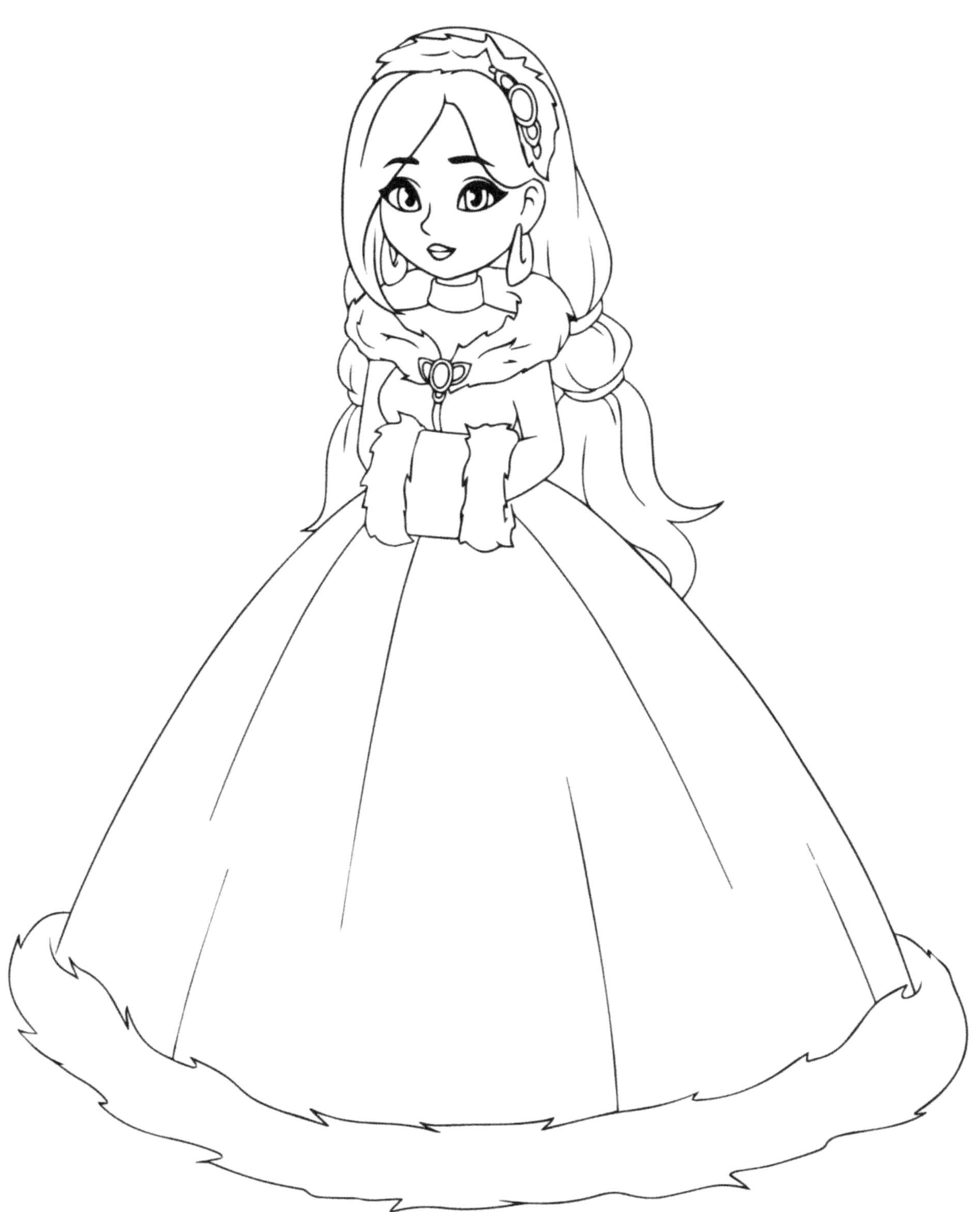

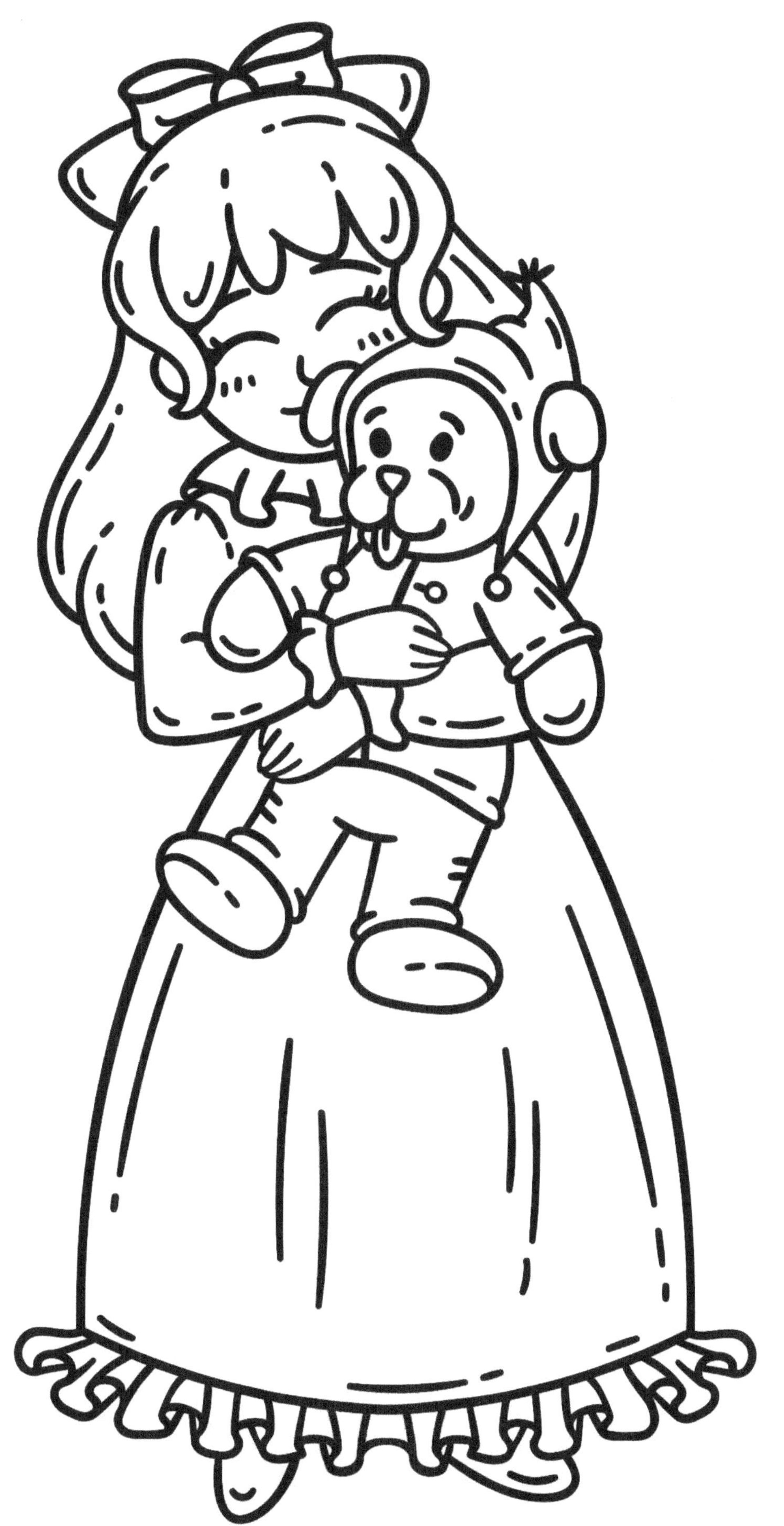

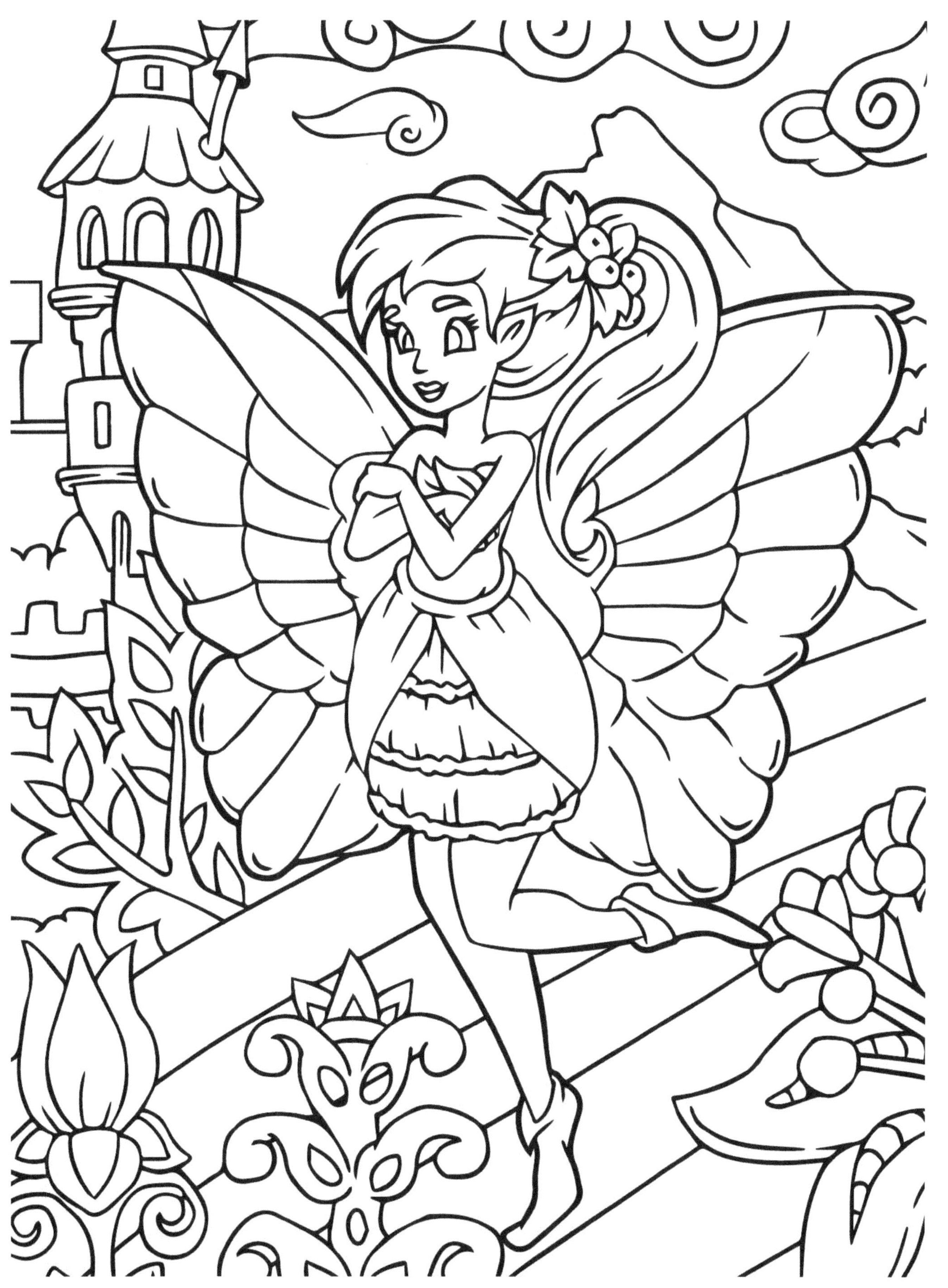

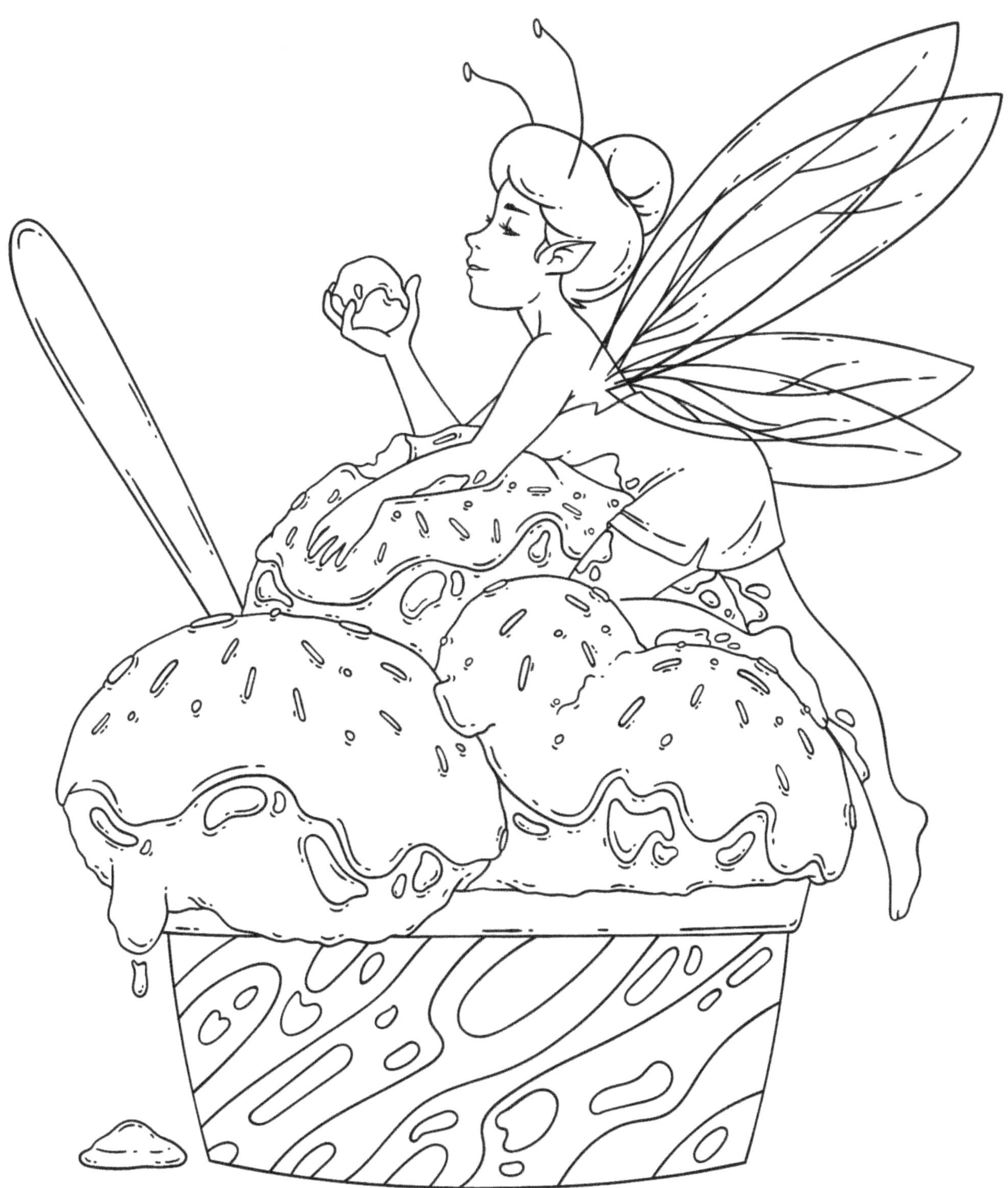

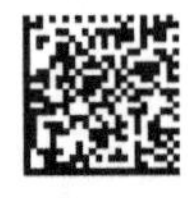
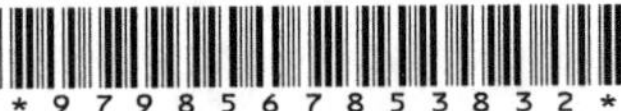